John Trivett Nettleship

Essays on Robert Browning's Poetry

John Trivett Nettleship

Essays on Robert Browning's Poetry

ISBN/EAN: 9783337138912

Printed in Europe, USA, Canada, Australia, Japan

Cover: Foto ©Thomas Meinert / pixelio.de

More available books at **www.hansebooks.com**

ESSAYS

ON

ROBERT BROWNING'S

POETRY

BY

JOHN T. NETTLESHIP

LONDON

MACMILLAN AND CO.

1868

LONDON: PRINTED BY
SPOTTISWOODE AND CO., NEW-STREET SQUARE
AND PARLIAMENT STREET

PREFACE.

In an age when knowledge, for its own sake, is by a large class of men as eagerly sought as gold, some apology seems necessary for a composition which professedly avoids facts, and deals in speculation. More especially would this apology seem to be due from anyone attempting to handle the works of a master, the beneficence of whose genius has led him to range in fields of knowledge so wide, and for their own sake to store harvests of learning so plenteous. Any such apology as may be due on this ground I am willing to make; but I should fail in my duty of respect were I to stop there, and refrain from expressing, though in feeble words, the extent of my debt in another way.

The life and the passion, the sin and exaltation, of men and women—all the beauty which thrills us in everything human because of its humanity—

form together a study beyond the mental grasp of
all save a few great and loving souls.

If, without fearing the charge of adulation, one
may add to the list of these the name of Robert
Browning; if we may affirm that wide and ripe as is
his learning, his highest glory is the unflinching zeal
with which he has mastered and given to the world
the results of human strife, toil, and achievement, I
do not fear to maintain such a conclusion; and
while acknowledging the profundity of his research,
I still venture to pay the dearer tribute, due from my
soul to his, of recording here the purpose and the
love which have been awakened in one man's life, not
by the consciousness that the poet knew so much,
but by the overmastering truth of those delinea-
tions of human strength and weakness, those strong
and tender warnings and encouragements, which
have times out of number intensified the desire for
truth and right, cheered despondencies, and sweet-
ened triumphs.

CONTENTS.

ESSAYS

ON

BROWNING'S POETRY.

INTRODUCTION.

IT is not my purpose in the following Essays
to enter into any criticism in the usual sense of the
word; that is, in the sense of an examination of
the merits or demerits of artistic style. Nor will
this be the place to speak of the poet in comparison with other poets present or past. That
much is to be said in the way of criticism of style
and of comparison with other poets I do not
deny; but there is so much important thought of
another kind to be worked out in a study of his
books, by the process of interpretation, that I could
not within reasonable limits handle both criticism
and interpretation without sacrificing the latter in
an undue degree. Again, considering that no poet
of the present day has worked in so wide a field,
it would at first sight seem the imperative duty of

B

the essayist to look at the poems in their historical aspect, and enter into a careful treatise on the various sources of knowledge from which Browning has derived his subjects. But to do this worthily one would have to fill volumes; and our more immediate concern is to show results, not seek for causes; to remind the world of the force of the man's brain who has so laboured, not examine into proofs which we may well accept on his authority.

Let me therefore, by way of introduction, state merely such results of (I hope) a careful observation as may perhaps help those who may choose to become students of Browning to arrive at definite conclusions as to his merits, and as may be necessary to explain the mode in which the main subjects of these Essays will be treated.

Looking at all his works in the four volumes in which they are at present published, we find that he has written no single poem or piece, except 'Christmas-eve' and 'Easter-day,' which does not profess to be more or less dramatic in its nature; for although we do not overlook the careful subdivision of his first volume into 'Lyrics,' 'Romances,' 'Men and Women,' we are reminded in a note at the beginning of that volume that its contents are 'always dramatic in principle, and so many utterances of so many imaginary persons,' not the poet's.

Now, though this dramatic quality is so observable, it must be admitted that, vivid as his portraits are, and great as is his power in delineating all human passion, there is no poet the fabric of whose works is so invariably sustained by a master-thread of subjectiveness. I shall not in this place give examples to prove this, because a perusal of any one of the plays (which from their nature are dramatic), and a comparison of it with any of the most professedly subjective pieces, will show the reader such a strong individuality of thought common to both as must at once convince him of the truth of the foregoing remarks.

But it would be culpable to omit from such a discussion as the present some mention of certain salient characteristics which are plainly discernible in everything the poet has written.

For instance, no one can fail to be struck by his overwhelming sense of the actual existence of a personal God, who rules men's souls, not by moral laws applicable to (what we may for the present purpose call) right and wrong in this life, but by rewards and punishments dealt to such souls, according as they shall develop themselves through all their successive stages of existence.

And when we have completely mastered that idea as displayed in all his deepest thoughts, we

are scarcely surprised to find, in connection with
or as a result of it, his firm-rooted belief that a
man's business on this earth is to learn the actual
extent of his own soul's powers, and having learned
them to develop them straightforward, not relatively to the moral or social laws prevailing in this
life, but absolutely for the soul's aggrandisement
hereafter.

The form which these ideas take in the poet's
mind is very plainly the result of his almost superhuman love for every form of life, animate or inanimate, in this earth ; a love so intense that one is
tempted to believe the man has actually in his
nature the sympathies and attributes of every form
of life he sings about; a love which is blended
with and relies upon a very noble sensuousness, displaying itself in two forms: the one being a special
physical sensuousness evidenced by the peculiar
sympathy which his writings express for bodily
strength, sexual passion, and all forms of physical
beauty, whether connected with or apart from
sexual passion; and the other being a special intellectual sensuousness evidenced by his peculiar
sympathy for art of all kinds, more particularly
music and painting.

And if we are almost awestruck by the force of
his love for the display of strength of all kinds,

whether of the body or the mind (a love which is after all the necessary consequence of the rest of his qualities); if we are startled almost by the hearty goodwill he evinces towards all persistence of endeavour, whether the object of that persistence be good or evil according to moral or religious standards, we are drawn strongly into sympathy with him in his keen love for humanity as such, a love which is displayed towards weakness and evil as much as towards strength and goodness, provided only the attribute be human; a divine sympathy, mixed with a beautiful kindly humour, which extends itself especially to the religious element in man, and which perhaps is nowhere else so strongly developed as in George Eliot's writings.

Such are the main features, more or less plainly displayed, which characterise all of Browning's writings. I have mentioned them thus particularly in this place, because it is necessary to remember them in considering the working of the poet's mind, and particularly in any attempt to arrive at a conclusion on the value of the thoughts worked out in the poems we are to discuss.

Having thus marked out in broad outlines the nature of the mind with which we have to deal, it is expedient to lay down the plan on which we are to proceed, to describe plainly the range of subjects which will be treated, and to indicate the nature of the thoughts on which we are to be occupied.

Since we have laid aside all criticism as such, whether artistic or comparative, and have freely trusted our author on the ground of history; since we are to examine the conclusions to be fairly drawn from the work placed before us as the result of the author's research, and not the form into which he has thrown it; the method of our examination will be throughout more or less analytical in its character, and will deal with the working of the impulses of the men and women portrayed in a few of his more powerful productions.

The subjects treated will be a few poems from the volume called ' Lyrics,' ' Romances,' ' Men and Women,' and the poem ' Sordello.'

In looking through the volume called ' Lyrics,' ' Romances,' ' Men and Women,' the student is at first bewildered, not only by the number of subjects handled, but also by the wide range of learning from which the poet has drawn his ideas.

It becomes absolutely necessary, in order to obtain a complete view of the whole, to marshal the poems on some plan of division under which they can be looked at with reference to each other. Their arrangement in the book is at present one of a purely artistic kind : but whether the reader desires to master them all for his own behoof, or proposes to write upon them a series of essays like the present, he must for the time disregard that arrangement, and mass the subjects of them under their different heads.

By far the larger portion numerically of the poems contained in this volume have for their subject the passion of men for women, and of women for men.

Several longer poems of great value deal with art in all its branches; and these are specially interesting because they deal, not with the great names which have become household words, but with earlier and obscurer representatives of the different arts—men whose work was the foundation of the masterpieces which are now world-renowned —men who, desiring no fame, were content to begin the building which is praised by the world as the work of their successors. And whether we travel back to listen to the early music of Italy and Germany; whether we stand reverently before the forgotten frescoes of Florence and the old Catholic churches ; whether we mourn with ' Pictor Ignotus,' yearn with 'Andrea del Sarto,' enjoy with ' Fra Lippo Lippi,' or ponder on the striving philosophy of ' Cleon,' we feel after each study that all these are

worthy to be learned by heart, as bygone builders
of a grand temple, and have been nobly and
worthily remembered by their brother of the nineteenth century.

Religion, too, in its most bigoted as well as its
most liberal forms, is ably handled; from the Old
Testament of the Jews, from the effect of the after
development of the Christian religion, down to the
modern scepticism of Bishop Blougram, a fund of
powerful thought is evolved which is of incalculable
use for estimating religion in its historical bearings.

The subjects of patriotism and party and the
early dawn of learning, give scope to some of the
poet's noblest utterances.

In all these special subjects that peculiarly subjective mode of treatment which has before been
alluded to gives to each of the portraits a sort of
mannerism, which appears not only in the mode of
treating the accessories, but even in the cast of
expression. The thoughts in Saul (a poem dealing
with the early times of the Jewish monarchy) are
strongly tinged with the wide liberality of the poet's
own religious views; so are those in 'Karshish,'
'Master Hugues of Saxe-Gotha,' and 'Cleon.'

This is perhaps more especially the case where
the subject is one in which religion forms a part;
whatever the date of the story may be, the impulse

seems irresistible to add to the probable thoughts of the *dramatis persona* the possible thoughts which, were he as far seeing as the poet himself, at this day, would have arisen out of his actual knowledge and been prompted by his hypothetical aspirations.

But whatever loss may be thus sustained in the absolute truth of the portraiture is more than counterbalanced by the many new views which are presented, and by the lessons, always valuable, which one may learn from the artist's expression of the characteristics of his subject.

Now, besides the subjects which have been already indicated, this volume contains several poems which do not come under any one head, and which, as might be expected, are professedly of a more subjective and abstract nature.

Of this class there are some few which perhaps possess higher importance than all the rest. For while the poems to which we have alluded concern themselves with special classes of men, special modes of thought or worship, these so-called subjective poems deal with hopes, fears, and struggles, common to all men as human beings. And the depth and the width of the thought contained in these, and their actual practical value as setting forth views of life which may be actually worked out by any man, give them in the eyes of any one who professes to be in earnest an inestimable value.

Passing over several small pieces which seem almost purely subjective, such as ' Earth's Immortalities,' ' De Gustibus,' 'My Star,' we notice a few which may be classed as treating of social life. These are ' Up at a Villa,' 'A Pretty Woman,' ' Before and After,' 'A Light Woman;' two or three which, without coming under the head of art as a subject, have an artistic tendency, namely, 'Women and Roses,' ' Englishman in Italy,' ' Artemis Prologises;' two of historical interest, 'My Last Duchess' and ' Protus;' and three stories, ' The Glove,' ' The Pied Piper of Hamelin,' and ' The Flight of the Duchess.' Lastly there are three which unite with their subjective character an analytical spirit, namely, ' Instans Tyrannus,' ' Waring,' and ' Childe Roland,' and it is to the two latter of these that the remarks just made apply in particular.

In choosing from among this mass of subjects those pieces which seem to present the widest surfaces for examination, one naturally selects such as are best adapted for the proposed method of treatment ; that is to say, those whose artistic or historical aspect, being their least important part, can best dispense both with technical criticism and with any examination into the grounds of knowledge on which the poet based them.

In the artistic point of view the poems generally may be and have been handled by abler men
than myself; in the historical or scientific view, it
is competent to anyone to examine them for himself with far more minuteness than would be com-
patible with the size of a work like the present.

But when we consider that of all living poets we
are dealing with the profoundest thinker; when we
see what a wide and life-giving philosophy he pro-
mulgates; we shall agree that for actual use of all
men, whatever their mode of life, it is more important to evolve thoughts than to trace beauties
or faults of construction—more useful to discover
lessons for actual life than to examine historical
evidences.

The following essays then will deal entirely with
such poems and such poems only as present in
connection with their subject some view which,
apart from the accessories of time and place, is of
value either for abstract thought or for moulding
our own lives upon.

Taking the subjects under which the poems in
this volume have been arranged in the foregoing
pages, a selection will be made first from those
whose subject is the passion of love, either in man
or woman, and, secondly, from a few of the sub-
ective or analytical poems.

POEMS ON LOVE.

THESE are remarkable for their perfectly simple, natural tone, and for their freedom from that quality, strongly displayed in recent publications, which by many able critics has been condemned as morbid sensuality.

Now, although it is far from my purpose to enter into any critical comparison of the poems just now under discussion with similar poems of other writers either of the present or of former times, it is only fair to remark in passing that whatever merits may be possessed by other amatory effusions, not only on the score of beauty of colouring and expression, but of their courageous liberation of the art of poetry from trammels of prudery, the subjects of this essay are marked by a singular clearness and force of drawing, a distinct form, as well as a beauty of colour, which contrasts very favourably with past and contemporary writings, and, while always steering clear of uncleanness, is perfectly open and unashamed.

It is a strong male spirit which has dictated

these utterances. A spirit always the master and never the slave of passions which may be made either gracious or bestial; a spirit which, having true courage, is never afraid to speak out those things which, in his healthy and unwarped judgment, ought in the interests of humanity and art to be spoken freely.

Of the poems whose subject is the passion of love, about two-thirds represent the feeling of the man and one-third the feeling of the woman. We notice that the feeling of the man may be classed broadly under two heads.

The first comprises the more ordinary cases, where the man's thought does not go beyond this life, in respect of love, and where even in this life the love takes up his whole brain, seeming absolutely the best and only thing he can possess, without reference to anyone except himself; where, in fact, love in its consuming selfishness exalts itself over all other phenomena for no reason assigned; and this sort is divided into successful and unsuccessful love.

The effect of successful love in different men under different circumstances is shown in 'Meeting at Night,' 'Love among the Ruins,' 'Another Way of Love,' 'In Three Days,' 'Mesmerism,' 'In a Gondola,' 'Porphyria's Lover.'

The effect on different men of failure in love, whether from the indifference, pique, or misunderstanding of their mistress, is shown in 'The Lost Mistress,' 'Lover's Quarrel,' 'Misconceptions,' 'A Serenade at the Villa,' 'One Way of Love,' 'Love in a Life,' and 'Life in a Love,' 'Time's Revenges,' 'Rudel to the Lady of Tripoli.'

Under the second head, we see how men of high intellect, whether they fail or succeed in love, find in their power of loving more use than actual present enjoyment, and are compelled by their aspiring nature to search for causes and effects, for the good their love may do, for its use here or hereafter.

Of those who succeed, three instances are given; those namely, which are described in 'By the Fireside,' 'Respectability,' and 'One Word more.'

Of those who fail, the utterances are to be found in 'Cristina,' 'Evelyn Hope,' 'The last Ride together,' and 'Two in the Campagna.'

It should be noticed that male jealousy is not treated at all.

The feeling of the woman as represented in those poems which depict the passion of women, has a less wide range, and though not so clearly marked out in divisions, may also be classed under the heads of failure and success.

The effect on the woman of her love being reciprocated is instanced in 'The Confessional,' 'Parting at Morning,' 'Woman's Last Word,' 'Any Wife to any Husband,' 'Count Gismond.'

The effect on the woman of that love being despised or thwarted is only twice delineated, namely, in 'The Laboratory' and 'In a Year.'

There remain two love poems which either as stories or dialogues, or in their mode of treatment, deal with the mutual love of a man and a woman. These are 'In a Gondola,' and 'The Statue and the 'Bust.'

In none which relate to the woman do we observe the width of view and intellectual power which are attributed to the male lover; and the only poem in which anything beyond the actual love of this life is even imagined is 'Any Wife to any Husband ;' but even here the range of thought is not so wide as it is in 'Evelyn Hope,' for instance ; though there is some sort of kindred in the thoughts of each.

In all the poems which relate to the feelings of the man under the first head, we observe that however beautiful the ideas expressed, the mind is influenced wholly by a selfishness which shows itself in utter want of appreciation of any state of circumstances other than that in which the speaker finds himself.

But in those which relate to the man's feelings under the second head there is a width of view, a power of grasp, which has probably never before been so forcibly portrayed.

In the poems which relate to the woman's feelings we notice principally (where her love is returned) an absorption of her spirit into that of the man, a blind clinging to some idea of God as formed through education and association merely, and an absolute want of originality and of power to look at the passion of love in an abstract sense, outside the woman herself and her lover.

These distinctions are worth noticing because of the importance of the subject in present social life.

One may fairly presume that in giving us portraits of selfish love the poet intended us to see not only how beautiful, how eloquent, is the passion, but also that the selfishness of it is in general a fatal drawback to its influence as a useful thing: that unless there is the elevating power of some hope beyond the actual personal gratification, the love, however consuming, however ideal, is more or less of a pernicious influence, paralysing or imprisoning all the other powers.

But the few poems in which men are swayed by love in its widest and most far-reaching sense, deal with the passion as something outside the

speaker, whose existence as a force in the world
to be used for good or for evil he recognises just as
clearly as he recognises any other force or power
of brain.

And although by the majority of artists, whether
of past or present times, love is usually treated as
a praiseworthy thing, to which all other feelings
may lawfully be sacrificed ; although even the most
self-sacrificing lovers are rarely practically unselfish,
either in fiction or real life; and although few men
are capable of looking as calmly at the subject of
their own love as the speaker in ' Evelyn Hope,' or
in ' By the Fireside '—simply because these are
men of exceptional power—still the teaching contained in the poems before us is valuable to us all,
as setting up an ideal to which any man may at
least strive to approach.

Let us now select some few poems whose profundity, obscurity, or wideness of range, afford the
best materials for our speculation.

We shall confine our attention to those poems
which treat of the man's feelings under the second head already mentioned. Of these ' Cristina,'
' Evelyn Hope,' ' The Last Ride Together,' may
well be considered in conjunction ; while ' By the
Fireside,' ' Respectability,' and ' One Word More,'
form a second trio which also present a continued

train of thought. One poem already mentioned, dealing with the woman's feelings, 'Any Wife to Any Husband,' also deserves special notice.

'Cristina,' 'Evelyn Hope,' and 'The Last Ride Together,' present three pictures of three different men who have accepted their fate as failing to achieve the gratification of their passion. In the first and last the lovers fail by reason of their mistresses' misappreciation; in 'Evelyn Hope' the speaker mourns over the death of a girl whom he loved, but who died before she was old enough to understand his love.

As all three will bear explanation, it will be well to consider the actual subject of each in turn, and then to look at them together as a group of studies not only very interesting in themselves, but also possessing a further purpose of actual teaching.

'Cristina' comes first in the book, and is a lyric of considerable beauty in its wording and rhythm.

At first reading it seems a slight fugitive piece to be passed by with a comment on its grace and beauty, or its idle dreaminess. But on looking closer into the nature of the man who speaks in it we shall find thought fit for a lifetime.

The image of the man rises before us, as one who not only fails here, there, and everywhere in things of this life, but who perhaps boasts of not one true friend. **In** his huddled ungraceful pose, and odd but not unkindly face, one sees by time a strange dumb yearning, showing **the need for sympathy from without.** Men and girls pass unheedful, or perhaps noticing him only with a gentle scornful pity. But one girl he sees—Ah, that moment! not counted in the years; **not** remembered as on such a day of such **a** year; but standing by itself, a white gleaming flame in the darkness of a lonely life.

The man, hitherto **used to groping in darkness,** will hereafter, in **his** weariest **moments, turn to** that flame to **keep in** use his **faculty of sight.** The thought which the girl's face **kindled in him** thus finds utterance **in speech:**

I.

> She should never have looked at me
>   If she **meant I** should **not love her!**
> There are plenty . . . men, **you call such,**
>   **I suppose . . . she may discover**
> All her soul to, if she pleases,
>   And yet leave much as she found them:
> But **I'm not so,** and she knew it
>   **When she** fixed me, glancing round them.

.

'At last,' he cries, ' in **this jostle** of brutal men and women, I feel one gentle healing touch, which will soothe my remembrance **for ever. Not the** touch of one of those scornfully compassionate who

say, " How good to bestow oneself on this undeveloped barren man, and adorn his dreary life with
a pearl of love;" or (still worse), "I with my
strange yearning of sympathy, will lavish myself
on this poor block of humanity, and in my wealth
of nature give myself to be swallowed up in his all
receptive slough of stupidity." No! I am stupid
enough, but do I not know at least, if only by
moments, what my true endowments are? Surely,
too often, as I journey, a shock reminds me of the
false step, the blind guide, blindly followed; too
often a spark shows me all my failure, all my
desire. Nay, more; in lonely midnight watches, in
raging noonday battles, a feeling tells me often
that had I but followed an impulse here, a conscience there, all my waste would have been fertility.
But, alas! such impulses, such consciences, instead
of a guiding light, are ever a blazing fire which
burns to ashes the toil or the aspirations of years.'

III.

Oh, we're sunk enough here, God knows!
   But not quite so sunk that moments,
Sure tho' seldom, are denied us,
   When the spirit's true endowments
Stand out plainly from its false ones,
   And apprise it if pursuing,
Or the right way or the wrong way,
   To its triumph or undoing.

IV.

There are flashes struck from midnights,
  There are fire-flames noondays kindle,
Whereby piled-up honours **perish,**
  Whereby swoln ambitions dwindle,
While just this or that poor impulse,
  Which for once had play unstifled,
Seems **the sole** work of a lifetime,
  That away **the rest** have trifled.

And now, **not my** impulse, **not my** conscience, but (far **more** precious) another **soul,** comes **out** like a star from twilight to draw **me towards its** brightness. It is the star of love. With her **eyes,** she says to **me, 'We** are here in this world **for the** sake of love ; we came here through untold ages for that ; we shall go hence for **untold** ages having gained or lost that. But if, being **here for** the chance of love, we do not use it, we have lost it for ever; never **in the times to** come will a woman come to **you, or a man come to** me, to seek and find **it. Mayhap we** shall **have deeper blisses,** higher ends; **but not** that bliss, **not that** end !'

The light **of her** eyes which tells **me** this is **God's** secret; **but neither God nor devil shall wrench it from me.**

And now, whose is **the gain ? It** is mine; she knew this thing, but would **not** follow it to accomplishment. She has lost, I have gained, what we

both lived for. Her soul, her secret, are mine; in
the glory of her eyes I will walk secure, even to
the close—

> Life will just hold out the proving
>   Both our powers, alone and blended;
> And then, come the next life quickly!
>   This world's use will have been ended.

The words of 'Evelyn Hope,' like those of
'Cristina,' are the words of a dreamer; but the
utterance is wrung out of the sorrow of death; and
its keynote is a hope for the fulfilment of love
in other lives, not the knowledge of love in this
life. Cristina's lover was undeveloped, warped,
and unsuccessful; the mind of the speaker in
'Evelyn Hope' is already large and developed,
with aspirations beyond flesh and mortality, beyond the utmost hope of a fervent Christianity.
He, too, walks ever with the touch of God upon
his brow, under the brooding wings of God, who
keeps him safe from wounding; but while the
other seems morose and blockish, this man is
kindly, humorous, gay, sensuous. There is glowing
faith in his yearning:

III.

> Is it too late, then, Evelyn Hope?
>   What, your soul was pure and true,
> The good stars met in your horoscope,
>   Made you of spirit, fire and dew—

And, just because I was thrice as old,
   And our paths in the world diverged so wide,
Each was nought to each, must I be told?
   We were fellow mortals, nought beside?

IV.

No, indeed! for God above
   Is great to grant, as mighty to make,
And creates the love to reward the love :
   I claim you still, for my own love's sake!
Delayed it may be for more lives yet,
   Through worlds I shall traverse, not a few :
Much is to learn and much to forget
   Ere the time be come for taking you.

For that which God made good shall in the end
have its purpose in being good; and no least
earthly beauty, no little flower, no white sunray,
no gold hair, red mouth, pure brow, shall go un-
honoured to darkness and the grave :—

V.

But the time will come—at last it will,
   When Evelyn Hope, what meant, I shall say,
In the lower earth, in the years long still,
   That body and soul so pure and gay?
Why your hair was amber, I shall divine,
   And your mouth of your own geranium's red—
And what you would do with me, in fine,
   In the new life come in the old one's stead.

VI.

I have lived, I shall say, so much since then,
  Given up myself so many times,
Gained me the gains of various men,
  Ransacked the ages, spoiled the climes ;
Yet one thing, one, in my soul's full scope,
  Either I missed or itself missed me :
And I want and find you, Evelyn Hope!
  What is the issue ? let us see!

What is the issue ? Millions of years hence the imperial intellect, the boundless knowledge of that man grown pure, shall rise, twinned with the full crowned beauty of his love grown perfect, and draw into themselves those earthly beauties which sank to dust here, only to awake to immortal beauty beyond the stars.

VII.

I loved you, Evelyn, all the while!
  My heart seemed full as it could hold—
There was place and to spare for the frank young smile,
  And the red young mouth and the hair's young gold.
So, hush,—I will give you this leaf to keep—
  See, I shut it inside the sweet cold hand.
There, that is our secret! go to sleep ;
  You will wake, and remember, and understand.

'The Last Ride Together,' though a comparatively simple poem, is mentioned here because it seems to be in some sort a development of the ideas contained in the two former.

A man who has spent years in a passion for a
girl, is at last told he must hope no more. Possessed of that strength which eventuates under
failure in a strong cheerful fatalism, he has the
courage to crush down the rising despair, and ask
for a last ride with his mistress. A little favour to
grant ; but one which, with the grand imagination of
love, he makes the foundation of a boundless ideal :

II.

My mistress bent that brow of hers ;
Those deep dark eyes where pride demurs
When pity would be softening through,
Fixed me a breathing-while or two
    With life or death in the balance : right !
The blood replenished me again ;
My last thought was at least not vain :
I and my mistress, side by side,
Shall be together, breathe and ride,
So one day more am I deified—
    Who knows but the world may end to-night.

III.

Hush ! if you saw some western cloud
All billowy-bosomed, over-bowed
By many benedictions—sun's
And moon's and evening star's at once,
    And so, you, looking and loving best,
Conscious grew, your passion drew
Cloud, sunset, moonrise, star-shine too,
Down on you, near and yet more near,
Till flesh must fade for heaven was here !
Thus leant she and lingered—joy and fear !
    Thus lay she a moment on my breast.

In the bright air, with the blessed presence at his side, he turned resolutely, yet by no effort of will, to make the best of what he had done, what he lost:

IV.

Then we began to ride. My soul
Smoothed itself out—a long-cramped scroll
Freshening and fluttering in the wind.
Past hopes already lay behind.
  What need to strive with a life awry?
Had I said that, had I done this,
So might I gain, so might I miss.
Might she have loved me? just as well
She might have hated—who can tell?
Where had I been now if the worst befell?
  And here we are riding, she and I.

'I have given my life for love,' says he; 'I see statesmen, soldiers, poets, painters, musicians, who give their lives for patriotism and art. The statesman and soldier are rewarded by an epitaph which they never read; the artists fail, are poor, grow grey with striving, and in the end are no nearer their goal than those who have never started in the race. I, who gave my youth, at least have one desire fulfilled; for am I not riding with her? I at least have one last chance of drawing back from the gulf of despair into which I was fast rushing. And then—

IX.

Who knows what's fit for us ?   Had fate
Proposed bliss here should sublimate
My being ; had I signed the bond—
Still one must lead some life beyond,—
　Have a bliss to die with, dim-descried.
This foot once planted on the goal,
This glory-garland round my soul,
Could I descry such ?   Try and test !
I sink back shuddering from the guest—
Earth being so good, would Heaven seem best?
　Now, Heaven and she are beyond this ride.

If I had gained my ideal, should I have looked for
heaven ? Could I have died, as I shall die now,
with a hope beyond ?   Would heaven seem best, if
earth were so good ?   At least I retain that hope,
of heaven, and perhaps of her, in another life.

But, at the last the old earth hope comes stealing
back, as he looks again at her. How if that hope
of heaven, which a moment ago was formless and
vague, be an actual fulfilment ; how if that which is
his highest pleasure now, be destined to become,
from temporal, eternal—from weakness, strength—
from dimness, clearest vision ? How if this yearning
of his be the germ of a yearning ever fulfilled, the
same in kind, but infinitely magnified in degree,—

And Heaven just prove that I and she
Ride, ride together, for ever ride ?

Now these poems present us with three distinct notions or ideals of love. The first is that the *main* purpose for which each man and woman is born on this earth is to love some other woman or man, and that if that purpose is not carried out it will never be allowed gratification in any succeeding life. The second, assuming the existence of love in a man or woman, concludes that that love if honest will, though it fails of achievement here, be surely fulfilled in some future life. The third speaker creates a further ideal which is a development of the others. He has lost his hope here ; but while making the best of his loss, and contrasting himself favourably with other failing strivers, inasmuch as he gets something while they get nothing, he buoys himself with the hope that the highest bliss *may* be the change from the minute's joy to an eternal fulfilment of joy.

A close examination of these three views (whose seeming inconsistency we accept at first sight on the ground that three different men, three different sets of circumstances, are depicted) show us that there is a kind of unity between them.

The speaker in 'Cristina' lays down as an abstract proposition with regard to the purpose of our life here, that we must, or ought to at some time or other, call into action a faculty which until

so awakened lies dormant within us, the faculty of
loving. The speakers in 'Evelyn Hope' and 'The
Last Ride,' taking love as a thing existent which is
swaying them at the moment, and not being called
on by necessity of circumstances to seek for causes
why it should be there, simply create for themselves
out of their hopelessness here, and their desire of
fruition hereafter, two very high ideals. These
ideals, while harmonising with each other, do not
violate but rather carry out the principle of the
aspirations which moved Cristina's lover, in that
they fulfil the condition of the actual existence of
love in this life.

But while we observe this consistency of view in
utterances professedly dramatic; while we are glad
to find that the aspiration of each speaker perfects
and supplements the others ; we must not forget
an important element common to all three which
stamps them yet more decidedly with a unity of
purpose.

As has been observed before, in almost all the
poems on love, the simple gratification of the personal desire, however idealised, is the mainspring
of the thought. But the ideas in these three poems
are applied by each speaker (unconsciously perhaps) not only to himself and his love, but to the
loves of all humanity. At first sight it may seem

that their high hopes are the result of overweening
egoism. But if it be so, the egoism is but the
necessary consequence of genius, and while seeking
rewards for itself, seeks only from a deep sense of
justice, a feeling that what is meant to be fulfilled
in the particular case must in the end be fulfilled
under similar conditions in the case of every other
human being.

These are no selfish lovers, who can see no
further than their own individual entity; they each
and all, even while claiming the highest possible
boon, do in fact separate themselves from themselves, and without knowing it stand apart and
judge of their own passion as an actual existing
attribute common to all other men. Should we in
this sense consider their conclusions as one whole,
what use can we make of them when thus
blended?

If we believe with Cristina's lover that we are
here in this life, as distinguished from all other
lives before and after, for the purpose of loving
somebody; with Evelyn Hope's lover, that, having
fulfilled that condition here, we shall surely enjoy
it to the full in some future state; and with the
lover in ' The Last Ride,' that it is possible that
love enjoyed may be, not only one fulfilment of a
future state, but that fruition which is more glorious

and all-satisfying than any other, we do but in-
tensify powers of which we are assuredly possessed,
and by the very nature of our hopes for their
exercise, elevate and purify our desires.

Finding ourselves possessed of certain instincts,
whose development is the passion of love, and
which claim exercise in one way or another; finding, as a physical fact, that such instincts repressed
have almost universally a harmful effect, and therefore that within proper limits the exercise of them
is physically speaking an actual necessity; finding
that not only as reproductive agents are these instincts in themselves of incalculable importance, but
moreover, that in their exercise for that purpose
they expand our sympathetic powers, and nourish
and extend the power of action of our other attributes; we do but take another step, to learn first
that perhaps the passion is but a symbol of the
infinite yearning of a first cause, a type of that
boundless love which, wedded to boundless power,
has been imaged as the all-ruling Deity; and then
that this very passion, infinitely extended, may be
the means of our helping untold millions as God's
vicegerents in other existences.

And again, if we believe that, since the attribute
or power of loving exists in us, it exists for a purpose which, in the nature of things, must be satis-

fied by an object to work on ; if we believe that
no love which has honestly sprung up in any man's
breast can go unrewarded altogether, lest thereby
so much power be lost in the machine of the
universe; and if, following up this thought, we
see the possibility that that love which must be
rewarded somewhere because of its necessary use
as a working force, may be the very actual force
which shall sway planets and stars in boundless
eternities, where sin and suffering are not ; if we
thus dare to weld together the thoughts expressed
in these three poems, what a glorious picture is
unfolded to our view!

Who shall say whether the little germ of one
man's love truly begun, for one woman, may not
in some far away life arise an infinite passion, by
whose glowing impulse the two shall mount upwards, fashioning to themselves out of the unper-
fected instincts and lessons of former lives a knowledge always growing ? And if for many lives he
and she toil on, failing, learning, and accumulating
force for efforts always redoubled in strength—
surely at last, when learning is as the sea dried up,
and knowledge the mysteries of its depths laid bare,
the two will stand blended by their now boundless
passion into one transcendent being, in the sky of
perfect power. When labour and pain are over,

and division and duality are things of forgotten ages, the perfect human entity, taking throne at the foot of God, will wield the sceptre of power, instinct with the spirit of love, over the millions who are still toiling and climbing, and in the end the whole world will blend in the inconceivable splendour of a star that blazes through an ever-present eternity!

'By the Fireside,' 'Respectability,' and 'One Word More,' show us three men who have been successful in their passion, and present to us views of the use of love which, while less transcendental than those put forward in the three poems we have just been considering, are perhaps of more practical value for the working life of the present world.

'By the Fireside,' one of the most valuable poems in this volume, contains the history of two lives fused into one by the flame of love reciprocated; and while possessing high merits as an analytical study, is marked by a more obviously subjective character than most of the poet's works.

The speaker is a man who has been a citizen in many realms of knowledge, and has already passed the stormy spring-time of his youth. In one of

those golden hours which, as they pass, drop a
blessing on our prime of summer, he sits down by
the wayside; and casting his thoughts forward
into the future, prophesies what will employ his
reposing spirit when he has reached old age.

II.

I shall be found by the fire, suppose,
   O'er a great wise book as beseemeth age,
While the shutters flap as the cross-wind blows,
   And I turn the page, and I turn the page,
Not verse now, only prose !

III.

Till the young ones whisper, finger on lip,
   ' There he is at it, deep in Greek :
Now, then, or never, out we slip
   To cut from the hazels by the creek
A mainmast for our ship !'

IV.

I shall be at it indeed, my friends !
   Greek puts already on either side
Such a branch-work forth as soon extends
   To a vista opening far and wide,
And I pass out where it ends.

V.

The outside-frame, like your hazel-trees—
   But the inside archway narrows fast,
And a rarer sort succeeds to these,
   And we slope to Italy at last
And youth, by green degrees.

When he is old, he will, in thought, retrace the paths of knowledge he has trod, and he compares himself, in reference to the knowledge he will have acquired, to a traveller through a many-columned vista of a wood, who explores every path in it. The outside paths, which he will explore first, will show him the common English growths (hazel trees), namely the knowledge acquired in and from England. Each inner path will have rarer kinds of trees; the innermost of all, the rarest. When he shall have explored all the other paths, he will come at last to the innermost sanctuary of the wood's vista, and pursue that inner path alone, knowing the rest by heart. This innermost path is his own inner life; and pursuing it in retrospect, he will come to Italy, where his youth was spent, and at last reach the first beginning of his life, the moment when his own and his wife's spirits became first blended into one.

With a loving word in passing to that Italy, which seems in some sort to symbolise his own beloved, he pursues his train of thought. He will find himself once more on that very mountain path where his troth was plighted; and will tenderly con over all the things he saw there, seeing in each double meanings by the light of experience, and love enjoyed. He will see once more

the ruined chapel far up in the pass; a thing which
had, like himself, a pathetic past of its own, to
which he and his love, with an unknown future
before them, were proceeding.

Another step, and they two stood in the midst of
the great maker, nature; the power which dumbly
influences the little lives, the everlasting loves, of
men and women. The thread of water joyously
leaping over the ravages of the bygone storm-tor-
rent, typified those little lives lightly threading
their way through the destruction of past ages.
As that thread of water crept down to feed the
lake below, so *her* life moved onwards to feed and
blend with his; while above them earth's greatest
things (the mountains), meeting the eternal heaven
in purity, pointed whither small humanity might
aspire, and reach.

These two lives, separate as yet, went on by
a narrow path side by side. Close to them the
tender growths and reproductions of nature's earth
life clung to the ruins of past times, even as the
present of man is joined with the past of God, even
as the gracious deeds which may be done by man
will beautify a wilderness of sin.

At that point of his life he seemed to be entering an early autumn; his life's fruits, though—like
the chestnuts falling that day—they seemed to fall

almost too soon, might yet, like the creepers' crim-
son and gold leaf, beautifying the fairy needled
moss, be of use thereafter for grace and tenderness.
And as autumn had its sudden good growths of
one night—the mushrooms, shining pure amidst the
evil growths of the same night, the toadstools—so
that early autumn of his life might bear sudden
unlooked-for good fruits among the equally sudden
evil fruits of bad impulses.

He and his love came at last to the chapel, with
its pathetic past, standing in the midst of stagnation, which was to be the womb of two new births.

As the chapel stood in the midst of stagnation,
so his heart seemed to stand in the world, dead,
and longing to be revived. As the smallest midges
were not ashamed to grace with their dancing the
stagnation and lifelessness which surrounded the
chapel ; as the smallest growths of lichen and ivy
were not ashamed to beautify the chapel and its
surrounding rocks ; so no heart, however seemingly
lonely and sterile, is too useless for God ; He will
ever take care that in some way, hidden or revealed, it shall bear fruit, even though it be only
the fruit of being a joy perhaps to small unknown
beings, the fruit of being a stronghold on which small
creatures clinging may live and suck nourishment.

The chapel, too, whose old age was helpful to

the few low people who came to worship and get
comfort within it, symbolised the speaker's future old
age, and its hopeful use in experience and sympathy.

And as the chapel with its product of art, so the
speaker in the glow of his youth, had each stood
as a monument of the beginning of man's aspirations after beauty, and both still bore the marks of
their former glory. Now, all alone, the chapel was
left to the love of a single bird, was left to watch
over the stray sheep who came to drink at its pond,
and the poor men who came to drink their religious life at its altar. Thus the chapel left
alone with the bird and its song symbolised the
retirement of age, and the sympathy chord of
youth which would thrill through it.

And here he breaks off the thread of his thought
and takes up a new one.

XXI.

My perfect wife, my Leonor,
    Oh, heart my own, oh, eyes, mine too,
Whom else could I dare look backward for,
    With whom beside should I dare pursue
The path grey heads abhor?

XXII.

For it leads to a crag's sheer edge with them;
    Youth, flowery all the way, there stops—
Not they; age threatens and they contemn,
    Till they reach the gulf wherein youth drops,
One inch from our life's safe hem.

Why, says he, do I dare go so minutely, step by
step, over the path of my youth? Only because
it led to you, my love! In this my thought, I am
looking forward to a time of age when I shall have
to look back, and shall look back with joy, along
the path of my youth. To that path the majority
of those who are growing old, as I must do one
day, shun looking back at all. For they have
gone on blindly, they have never looked before
them into the future as I am doing now, so that
when they come to the end of youth, it is like
coming to the edge of a precipice at unawares. On
they go, heedless of or despising age, who threatens
them momently, till, for want of foresight, they and
their youth drop over into the gulf, when if they
had stopped an inch before, they and it would
have been kept safe through life.

XXIII.

With me, youth led—I will speak now,
   No longer watch you as you sit
Reading by firelight, that great brow
   And the spirit-small hand propping it,
Mutely, my heart knows how.

XXIV.

When, if I think but deep enough,
   You are wont to answer, prompt as rhyme;
And you, too, find without a rebuff
   The response your soul seeks many a time,
Piercing its fine flesh-stuff.

XXV.

My own, confirm me! If I tread
 This path back, is it not in pride
To think how little I dreamed it led
 To an age so blest that by its side
Youth seems the waste instead?

Now our two lives are one : no obstructing rocks
can stop the stream.

XXVII.

Think, when our one soul understands
 The great Word which makes all things new—
When earth breaks up and heaven expands—
 How will the change strike me and you
In the house not made with hands?

And when our two souls drawn into one stream,
come to the ocean of heaven, how will the change
strike us?

Still as we wander through that ocean, you will
be first to see in it, you will make me see, new
depths, new wonders. Could we have expected
this at first? But since it must and will be, nay, is
so, let me for very love come back to the beginning
and see how it has come about.

XXX.

Come back with me to the first of all,
 Let us lean and love it over again—
Let us now forget and now recall,
 Break the rosary in a pearly rain,
And gather what we let fall!.

I had lived my life much as that small singing
bird by the chapel lived, unheeding trouble save
when (like the hawks) it came in sight. But in
that early afternoon of my life (as it seemed), I,
like the bird, began to feel my heart convulsed with
the yearning to speak itself out. In that afternoon,
I found you. The rest of the world around me was
still, and you could hear my voice. We took the
mountain path, talking indifferently; we gave tender
regard to the old chapel with its past (in half
prophetic mood), and gave wonder to the moss,
whose deeper meaning is now so clear. We saw that
the chapel's precious things, like the precious things
of a man's life, and of my life, were locked out
of sight of the crowd of gazers and plagiarists;
and then we came back to our present moment.

XXXVII.

Oh moment, one and infinite!
  The water slips o'er stock and stone;
The west is tender, hardly bright;
  How grey at once is the evening grown—
One star, the chrysolite!

At that moment, and just as the brightness
seemed fading out of my life, just as it seemed to
be growing grey like the evening, one star arose to
bless it. I stood there alone, looking at my new
risen star momently brightening my heaven, whose

lights and shades throbbed around that star in
agony of yearning to blend with it. It was a
moment when a sound, a breath, more or less,
made all the difference between the blackness of
despair and the blinding glory of hope fulfilled.

XLI.

For my heart had a touch of the woodland-time,
    Wanting to sleep now over its best.
Shake the whole tree in the summer prime,
    But bring to the last leaf no such test :
' Hold the last fast ! ' runs the rhyme.

XLII.

For a chance to make your little much,
    To gain a lover and lose a friend,
Venture the tree and a myriad such,
    When nothing you mar but the year can mend !
But a last leaf—fear to touch !

XLIII.

Yet should it unfasten itself and fall
    Eddying down till it find your face
At some slight wind—(best chance of all)
    Be your heart henceforth its dwelling-place
You trembled to forestal !

I, in that early autumn time of my brain, stood
there like an old wood-god worshipping a nymph
changed to a tree, which tree had now shed all its
summer glory, and held but one last autumn leaf.
I knew that there was no chance for me to gain any
token of love from that tree, with its one precious

leaf, by any act of my own.   The tree must give
me its leaf or I must go lacking; I was not in that
summer prime when I could take by force of brain
what gifts I would.   But the tree was good to me.
At the slight wind of my unexpressed mad longing,
it unfastened its leaf and let it flutter into my
bosom, where it rests now.   In that moment, you
fulfilled my hope, and the heaven was complete
with its blended star.   What though the night
seemed to hide the heaven?   The heaven knew
that it held its star, and that was enough.   The
great maker nature had in her forests dumbly influenced our two little lives, and made them one.
Day by day since that time we have seen how
through that moment's product, through that thing
done by you and me, all that we see and know has
its full worth, all the world is in harmony with our
lives.   What we have done since is to love; thus
have we forwarded the general work of mankind;
and while recruiting the race by our efforts in
accordance with the great order, have lived our own
lives as well.

XLIX.

How the world is made for each of us!
How all we perceive and know in it
Tends to some moment's product thus,
When a soul declares itself—to wit,
By its fruit—the thing it does!

L.

Be Hate that fruit, or Love that fruit,
   It forwards the General Deed of man,
And each of the many helps to recruit
   The life of the race by a general plan ;
Each living his own, to boot.

LI.

I am named and known by that hour's feat ;
   There took my station and degree :
So grew my own small life complete
   As nature obtained her best of me—
One born to love you, sweet !

LII.

And to watch you sink by the fireside now
   Back again, as you mutely sit
Musing by firelight, that great brow
   And the spirit-small hand propping it
Yonder, my heart knows how !

LIII.

So the earth has gained by one man more,
   And the gain of earth must be heaven's gain too,
And the whole is well worth thinking o'er
   When the autumn comes : which I mean to do
One day, as I said before.

The piece called 'Respectability,' though very
short, is very significant :

I.

Dear, had the world in its caprice
   Deigned to proclaim, ' I know you both,
   Have recognised your plighted troth,
Am sponsor for you : live in peace !'

> How many precious months and years
>   Of youth had passed, that speed so fast,
>   Before we found it out at last—
> The world, and what it fears?

The idea expressed is that the independence of
thought and action which forms the necessary
groundwork for the making of a character, is incomplete unless it is itself founded upon the love
of a woman for the man, of a man for the woman,
begun and carried through in perfect indifference
to, and if need be defiance of, the laws of society.

II.

> How much of priceless life were spent
>   With men that every virtue decks,
>   And women models of their sex—
> Society's true ornament—
> Ere we dared wander, nights like this,
>   Thro' wind and rain, and watch the Seine,
>   And feel the Boulevart break again
> To warmth and light and bliss?

Had their love been first recognised by the
world, they, becoming by that recognition the
world's debtors, would have been compelled to
conform to its rules, all the while wearying their
strength by chafing under the restraint. But now
that the two have dared to do without that recognition, instead of passing many years of fruitless
striving against those fetters of conventionality

which, through their obligation to society and their ignorance of its weak points, they could not have broken save at the expense of years of toil, which would have wasted their powers, the two have had all the priceless years of their youth to spend in developing their true instincts, their pure and un-checked sympathies.

The beautiful lines called ' One Word More,' are addressed by the poet to his wife, and one feels almost afraid to touch them with the rude hand of the critic. If we speak of them reverently in a few words, it is because the thought of them, in its depth and sweetness, is a standing lesson to every artist. How graceful, how touching, is their open-ing music!

II.

Rafael made a century of sonnets,
Made and wrote them in a certain volume
Dinted with the silver-pointed pencil
Else he only used to draw Madonnas :
These, the world might view—but one, the volume.
Who that one, you ask? Your heart instructs you.
Did she live and love it all her life-time ?
Did she drop, his lady of the sonnets,
Die, and let it drop beside her pillow,
Where it lay in place of Rafael's glory,
Rafael's cheek so duteous and so loving—
Cheek, the world was wont to hail a painter's—
Rafael's cheek, her love had turned a poet's ?

III.

You and I would rather read that volume
(Taken to his beating bosom by it),
Lean and list the bosom-beats of Rafael,
Would we not? than wonder at Madonnas—
Her, San Sisto names, and her, Foligno,
Her, that visits Florence in a vision,
Her, that's left with lilies in the Louvre—
Seen by us and all the world in circle.

And then he tells us of Dante's attempt to draw an angel for Beatrice; and then—

VIII.

What of Rafael's sonnets, Dante's picture?
This : no artist lives and loves, that longs not
Once, and only once, and for one only
(Ah, the prize !), to find his love a language
Fit and fair and simple and sufficient—
Using nature that's an art to others,
Not, this one time, art that's turned his nature.
Ay, of all the artists living, loving,
None but would forego his proper dowry :
Does he paint? he fain would write a poem —
Does he write? he fain would paint a picture,
Put to proof art alien to the artist's,
Once, and only once, and for one only,
So to be the man and leave the artist,
Gain the man's joy, miss the artist's sorrow.

Every artist who lives and loves a woman, desires to honour her by employing some highest attribute of his nature (kept in the innermost holy of holies of the temple, sacred from the world) in order to produce a work which shall give her delight.

In so doing he gets for himself the delight of an exercise of faculty irresponsible to any critic save his own loving heart, unchallenged by any opinion save the fondest praise of his woman love.

And why does this exercise of such faculty yield him such pleasure, and why is such pleasure never realised by him in the exercise of his proper art? Because Heaven's gift, which impels his spirit in its art career, has ever an earthly alloy in it, the alloy of harsh criticism, of ungrateful carping, of brutish infidelity. It is this harshness, ingratitude, infidelity, which is so fatal to the honesty and truth of the artist's work, and cripples his best efforts. And it is the unreserved sympathy of a woman who loves him, which is the strongest talisman to keep him pure, and reinvigorate his brain, nerveless with much striving. Take an instance, not of an artist, but of a patriot.

IX.

He who smites the rock and spreads the water,
Bidding drink and live a crowd beneath him,
Even he, the minute makes immortal,
Proves, perchance, his mortal in the minute,
Desecrates, belike, the deed in doing.
While he smites, how can he but remember,
So he smote before in such a peril,

E

When they stood and mocked—'Shall smiting help us?'
When they drank and sneered—'A stroke is easy!'
When they wiped their mouths and went their journey,
Throwing him for thanks—'But drought was pleasant.'
Thus old memories mar the actual triumph ;
Thus the doing savours of disrelish ;
Thus achievement lacks a gracious somewhat ;
O'er importuned brows becloud the mandate,
Carelessness or consciousness, the gesture.
For he bears an ancient wrong about him,
Sees and knows again those phalanxed faces,
Hears, yet one time more, the 'customed prelude—
'How shouldst thou, of all men, smite and save us?'
Guesses what is like to prove the sequel—
'Egypt's flesh-pots—nay, the drought was better.'

When Moses first gave water to the thirsty Israelites, they were ungrateful first, and unbelieving in God's power shown through Moses. When he did that miracle again, how could *he* do it in pure faith, when he remembered *their* infidelity? How could *he* do it in honest purity of desire to help them, when he remembered *their* ingratitude? And again, he can never make the unfeeling crowd love him for his human sympathy; he can only make them obey him through fear, by his mysterious power as a prophet. Then, how refreshing, how purifying, how strengthening for his work in the world, to have one woman's face to love!

For her sake, he would give up all his power and prophethood, only to have the right to minister to her wants as a man. Nay, he would even envy the camel which kneels patiently down to be killed for her sake, in order that its little hoard of bitter water may be used to quench her thirst.

Reverting to the examples of **Dante** and **Rafael**, the poet says :—

XII.

> I shall never, in the years remaining,
> Paint you pictures, no, nor carve you statues,
> Make you music that should all express me ;
> So it seems : I stand on my attainment.
> This of verse alone, one life allows me ;
> Verse and nothing else have I to give you.
> Other heights in other lives, God willing—
> All the gifts from all the heights, your own, love !

And yet I may do something here, if not in Rafael's way, at any rate in my own way, for my love.

For as a fresco painter will for his love's sake curb his hand and become illuminator to adorn her missal, so I, who have soared as dramatist, epoist, analyst, and lyrist, may write you these tender verses untouched, unaltered, **because** they are prompted by my great love.

Let then my labour as an artist be for all men my untouched words, straight from the brain and the heart, are for you.

Let my manner of speech be worked out and

polished for all **my** common **works**; for you **the**
very poverty of my speech will **endear it to you,**
because love prompted it.

And then, to return to my old conceit: see
the moon yonder! Suppose she loved a mortal;
would she show him **the** side she showed the world?
No! she would show him a new side—

> Side unseen of herdsman, huntsman, steersman,
> Blank to Zoroaster on his terrace,
> Blind to Galileo on his turret,
> Dumb to Homer, dumb to Keats—him, even!
> Think, the wonder of the moonstruck mortal—
> When she turns round, comes again in heaven,
> Opens out anew for worse or better?
> Proves she like some portent of an iceberg
> Swimming full upon the ship it founders,
> Hungry with huge teeth of splintered crystals?
> Proves she as the paved-work of a sapphire
> Seen by Moses when he climbed the mountain?
> Moses, Aaron, Nadab, and Abihu
> Climbed and saw the very God, the Highest,
> Stand upon the paved-work of a sapphire.
> Like the bodied heaven in his clearness
> Shone the stone, the sapphire of that paved-work,
> When they ate and drank and saw God also!

XVII.

> What were seen? None knows, none ever shall know.
> Only this is sure—the sight were other,
> Not the moon's same side, born late in Florence,
> Dying now impoverished here in London.
> God be thanked, the meanest of his creatures

Boasts two soul-sides, one to face the world with,
One to show a woman when he loves her.

Even so do I by you, even so does every artist
by his love.

Even so, too, do you, my moon, for me.

You, who having the praise of the world too,
can yet show me new beauties which the world
never can know ;

Thus they see you, praise you, think they know you.
There, in turn I stand with them and praise you,
Out of my own self, I dare to phrase it.
But the best is when I glide from out them,
Cross a step or two of dubious twilight,
Come out on the other side, the novel
Silent silver lights and darks undreamed of,
Where I hush and bless myself with silence.

XIX.

Oh, their Rafael of the dear Madonnas,
Oh, their Dante of the dread Inferno,
Wrote one song—and in my brain I sing it,
Drew one angel—borne, see, on my bosom !

The lovers in 'Cristina,' 'Evelyn Hope,' and
'The Last Ride Together,' spoke of love as an
aspiration which was not to be realised here at all,
but must have its completion in some other life.
Failure created in them their ideals; and what
the possible development, and how splendid the
consummation of such ideals, we have seen.

Dreams, alas! are too often the result of some thwarting of an object; but how ravishing in its unreality is the fantastic beauty of a dream!

The lovers who speak in 'By the Fireside,' 'Respectability,' and 'One Word More,' have succeeded, and are wedded to their loves; and their dreams, though beautiful, are less unreal and less fanciful. There is too, at first sight, less inconsistency between the ideas of each, than in those of the other three; for each is turning to actual use the same possession, the same fulfilment. But though the selfishness of success is a stronger trial to purity than the selfishness of failure, these large-hearted men do not fail to see the true use of their love, both for themselves and for others.

The speakers in 'By the Fireside,' and in 'Respectability,' have the same end in view, namely, how to use each his own and his mistresses' attributes for the widest good.

The speaker in 'One Word More,' adds to those of the others, in its full beauty, the ideal of the artist. All of them acknowledge that the love which has been blessed by enjoyment, is not to be used for selfish ends, but for widening of sympathy: and that just as we cannot complete our nature here without exercising the faculty of love, so if we do exercise it at all, and successfully, it must be used to help us towards the far away height to which the faith of the failing spirits has lifted them; that whether their ideal is to come to pass or not, at least the fortunate ones on this earth should do their little human work to help on the great harmony of God's work above, and while blending love with power for the purpose of helping all who need it here, may hope that when death comes, they too may be translated to the seat where power and love are unchecked and unblinded by sins and shortcomings.

We have now discussed all the most important love poems whose subject is the feeling of the man. Those which speak of the feeling of the woman are of unquestionable importance too, as dramatic efforts; but in treating them analytically, and selecting such only as go beyond the province of dramatic portraiture, we are as before hinted reduced to one poem which, expressing a woman's feelings, at the same time shows any sort of ideality as connected with other lives of other women, or with other existences after death.

This poem is ' Any Wife to any Husband,' and general as is its title, it displays far deeper insight into the usual character of the passion of even high-minded men than is, we fear, possessed by most women of the present day.

As in the other cases, we will take the poem and describe it shortly.

A wife lies dying in her bed; her husband's hand is in hers, and her eyes are dim with the shadow of the wing of death. Their love has been whole and perfect in body and soul for years; but not so blind, not so unreasoning on her part, as to prevent her from seeing clearly, more clearly perhaps from out of the grave's darkness than in the daylight of life, what is her husband's weakness, what his strength.

I.

My love, this is the bitterest, that thou
Who art all truth, and who dost love me now
   As thine eyes say, as thy voice breaks to say—
Shouldst love so truly, and couldst love me still
A whole long life through, had but love its will,
   Would death that leads me from thee brook delay!

II.

I have but to be by thee, and thy hand
Would never let mine go, nor heart withstand
   The beating of my heart to reach its place.
When should I look for thee and feel thee gone?
When cry for the old comfort and find none?
   Never, I know : Thy soul is in thy face.

Though I faded, our two souls would see clearly their own beauty, and renew their power in the failing of the flesh. For we should both remember

whence our souls sprang; we should fear to dis-
honour God by mistrust in the darkness, having
safe our soul's spark, given from his immortal fire.
Then indeed you would be perfect and pure
through life, and then what plaudits would ring
from the next world, when, new winged and clean
from earthly stain, you sprang to the sky and to
the angels for new fellowship in perfect truth!

But now, with my earthly love gone from you,
how bitter is it that you, who are so true and
grateful that you treasure even the flowers of one
holiday, must sink into impurity; you, who can let
strange things remain strange, but having found
love once, can keep it through years, though it
was only awakened by one slight tune, one passing
glance; you who, if we had only once met and
parted, would, having loved me, do all gracious
things to keep my image in your memory.

IX.

But now, because the hour through years was fixed,
Because our inmost beings met and mixed,
    Because thou once hast loved me—wilt thou dare
Say to thy soul, and who may list beside,
 'Therefore she is immortally my bride,
    Chance cannot change my love, nor time impair.

X.

' So, what if in the dusk of life that's left,
 I, a tired traveller, of my sun bereft,

Look from my path when, mimicking the same,
The fire-fly glimpses past me, come and gone.
Where was it till the sunset? where anon
    It will be at the sunrise! what's to blame?'

XI.

Is it so helpful to thee? canst thou take
The mimic up, nor, for the true thing's sake,
    Put gently by such efforts at a beam?
Is the remainder of the way so long
Thou need'st the little solace, thou the strong?
    Watch out thy watch, let weak ones dose and dream!

Can you say, again, 'Because there is other beauty,
I can still enjoy it without failing from any allegiance to that great beauty who is dead; this is
no more than preferring to see pictures instead of
the bare wall; still the new beauty admired detracts nothing from the old beauty worshipped?'
Ah me! So it must be; I must myself see from
my heaven above how you so fail; must myself
allow you, nay authorise you, to steal from me all
the love and truth you gave me, and bestow it
on others. Love, then, again if you will; say you
were in a trance of grief and have awoke; speak
the words and give the looks to new women, which
are stamped with the image of the love wherewith
I glorified them. Still you are mine; false however
long, you must come back to me at last.

XVII.

Only, why should it be with stain at all?
Why must I, 'twixt the leaves of coronal,
  Put any kiss of pardon on thy brow?
Why need the other women know so much,
And talk together, ' such the look and such
  The smile he used to love with, then as now!'

If I could live longest, should I be so false?
Would I not glory to go into your very tomb and
sit there, seeing your face on its walls, the better that
they are so blank and bare? Did I not even want
more time to get you by heart, that when I too
came to die, I might be fitter to join you beyond
the grave? And you, who are the nobler of us
two, can you not take this faith to me as a trial,
and for very pride, keep it unsullied?

XXI.

Pride?—when those eyes forestal the life behind
The death I have to go through!—when I find,
  Now that I want thy help most, all of thee!
What did I fear? Thy love shall hold me fast
Until the little minute's sleep is past
  And I wake saved.—And yet it will not be!

There is a terrible and bitter truth in all this
dying reproach. Few men have such a sustaining
power of love as to keep them firm in resisting the
fleshly desires, when she who has idealised those
desires is dead. So long as there is a hope of

regaining a mistress or a wife who is still loved,
many a man will remain faithful; but it is only
one in a million who has faith enough to keep the
image in his heart after the body is gone, and by
the tender beauty of that image to charm away the
rising lusts which will claim gratification. 'The
desire of the man is for the woman, the desire of
the woman is for the desire of the man;' and every
true woman finds more than enough to fill her
imagination and her life in the passion which she
has inspired in, and the passion which has been
roused in her by, one man who has loved her and
whom she has loved, truly and wholly.

Looking at this poem as a powerful epitome of
the highest hopes and joys of womankind generally in connection with the passion of love, let us
ponder upon the manifestations so put forth of the
highest form of woman's passion for man.

We see that although less aspiring, it is purer;
though not so strong, it is longer lived; that as a
fitting complement to and support of the male love
which in its highest development is always struggling upwards, it stands in its mute humility a
type of that perfection which looks to one superior;
and it teaches the man that his purity and constancy should be firmly established before he dares
to assert supremacy over all nature.

This woman-love, into which doubt enters not, is a realisation here of that perfect faith which man struggles for ever and fails to find; it is a love which has done already what the man strives to do; for it ever works to do good to his nature as worthily representing the whole of humanity; is now as unselfish as he can ever hope to be even in his wildest dreams; and always strives to help him to become more pure and more perfect.

The real love of the man is never born until the love of the woman supplements it; for the first feeling, refine it as he will, is but lust made clean for a little; it is merely the desire for instant fruition.

But when the full abandonment and absorption into himself, the full faith and constancy of the woman's love is made plain to him, then he begins to see that there may be wider uses for his desires; that the highest ideal of the object of love is already manifested in the purity and sympathy of his mistress; and that as he strives more and more to reproduce that ideal in himself, he and his mistress may at last, not in the flesh but in the spirit, when her tender unaspiring love is absorbed into his winged passion, blend into one perfect creature which exercises its double yet united powers for the unspeakable gladness of all that has life.

THE FLIGHT OF THE DUCHESS.

THIS poem tells a simple story, which all men to
whom I have talked about it have professed themselves at a loss to unravel. And they are not
content with merely saying that it is unintelligible:
they lift up their hands at its ruggedness and want
of melody, and exclaim, Is this poetry? Did anyone ever see such barbarous rhymes? Is there
anything in it after all? Or is it merely a freak of
this uncouth mind, so cramped and cooped by the
exigencies, which must be respected sometimes, of
rhythm and rhyme, that it must needs let out all
its most fantastic moods in one stream, and once
for all relieve itself of an oppressive burden? To
answer such critics in speech has been impossible,
perhaps because the only answer is an indirect one.
But while writing about other and more musical
utterances of the Poet's, I feel the necessity, according to the plan of these Essays, of giving a word or
two in explanation of, and assigning a motive to,
this much-abused poem.

The story is laid in a northern principality (whose duke was a vassal of a Kaiser of Germany), which kept its rough simple traditions in its own wilds, long after the court had got a flavour of heraldry, luxury, and pageantry.

The speaker is an obscure retainer of the Duke, and is the son of an old huntsman of that Duke's father. The Duke of the story had taken for his Duchess a convent girl; and the poem concerns the flight of that Duchess, or rather her abduction by an old gipsy woman.

The speaker opens his story with a description of his lord's principality :—

> Ours is a great wild country:
> If you climb to our castle's top,
> I don't see where your eye can stop ;
> For when you've passed the cornfield country,
> Where vineyards leave off, flocks are packed,
> And sheep-range leads to cattle-tract,
> And cattle-tract to open chase,
> And open chase to the very base
> Of the mountain, where, at a funeral pace,
> Round about, solemn and slow,
> One by one, row after row,
> Up and up the pine-trees go,
> So, like black priests up, and so
> Down the other side again
> To another greater, wilder country,
> That's one vast red drear burnt-up plain,
> Branched through and through with many a vein

Whence iron's dug, and copper's dealt ;
Look right, look left, look straight before—
Beneath they mine, above they smelt,
Copper-ore and iron-ore,
And forge and furnace mould and melt,
And so on, more and ever more,
Till, at the last, for a bounding belt,
Comes the salt sand hoar of the great sea shore,
—And the whole is our Duke's country !

The speaker goes on to tell how, when the old Duke had an heir, he was summoned by the Kaiser to present himself at court ; how he obeyed the summons, and how at the end of a year, sinking beneath the tedium of pomp and etiquette, the old rough Norseman sickened and died.

When he died, his Duchess left the principality (where she had managed her husband's affairs during his lifetime) and took the infant Duke with her to Paris.

At last, back she came, bringing with her the young Duke, now grown to manhood.   But his life at Paris had transformed him into a pert little elf, with all sorts of strange notions about the glory of his northland home, the virtues and heroic mould of his ancestors and subjects.   He set to work to dig up and exhibit to a wondering world a quantity of fossil observances of venery and middle age manners.   He perpetually worried his retainers' souls out of patience by his horrible usages and costumes :—

> And chief in the chase his neck he perilled,
> On a lathy horse, all legs and length,
> With blood for bone, all speed, no strength ;
> — They should have set him on red Berold,
> With the red eye slow consuming in fire,
> And the thin stiff ear like an abbey spire!

At last the time came that he must marry; and a lady was chosen for him, who had lived her life in a convent, but who was young, loving, and beautiful.

She was a woman, says the speaker, with a great loving heart, born to be the wife of a man to whom she could be helpful and cheering; but here, alas! she had nothing to do but sit and look stately; for had not this ape of a Duke, in his rage for middle age romancing, got an officer here, there, and everywhere? Was not everything done by rule and precedent? What on earth could the poor little warm girl do but pine in her ghastly splendour and die of it at last?

This gradual pining of hers, though it sorely irritated the Duke and his mother, was treated by them with the patronising superiority with which grown-up people sometimes treat the humours of a

F

fractious child, for whom a fit punishment will be found in due time.

Well, one autumn, the Duke having looked into his books found that the proper thing to do was to have a hunting party. He vexed his household's life with getting up the proper costumes ; and when he had settled everyone's part, his own included, it occurred to him to search for some rule ordaining the Duchess's duty. He found one at once :—

> When horns wind a mort and the deer is at siege,
> Let the dame of the castle prick forth on her jennet,
> And with water to wash the hands of her liege
> In a clean ewer with a fair towelling,
> Let her preside at the disembowelling.

This settled, the Duke signified to the poor little Duchess his wish that she should play her part in the masquerade. But she, weighed down, poor thing, beneath ceremony and pomp, and with little spirit left for anything but moping, begged to be excused. And what wonder ? Quoth the speaker (a sportsman himself)—

> Now, my friend, if you had so little religion
> As to catch a hawk, some falcon-lanner,
> And thrust her broad wings like a banner
> Into a coop for a vulgar pigeon ;
> And if day by day, and week by week,
> You cut her claws, and sealed her eyes,

And clipped her wings, and tied her beak,
Would it cause you any great surprise
If, when you decided to give her an airing,
You found she needed a little preparing?
—I say, should you be such a curmudgeon,
If she clung to the perch, as to take it in dudgeon?
Yet when the Duke to his lady signified,
Just a day before, as he judged most dignified,
In what a pleasure she was to participate,—
And, instead of leaping wide in flashes,
Her eyes just lifted their long lashes,
As if pressed by fatigue even he could not dissipate,
And duly acknowledged the Duke's forethought,
But spoke of her health, if her health were aught,
Of the weight by day and the watch by night,
And much wrong now that used to be right,
So, thanking him, declined the hunting,—
Was conduct ever more affronting?
With all the ceremony settled—
With the towel ready, and the sewer
Polishing up his oldest ewer,
And the jennet pitched upon, a piebald,
Black-barred, cream-coated, and pink eye-ball'd,—
No wonder if the Duke was nettled!

So he handed her over to his hell-cat of a mother to be scolded. And a scolding she got with a vengeance; which perhaps made her more obstinate, for she must have had a little pride left. So the Duke, not to be baulked, sallied forth on his hunting party, to do without the towel and ewer as best he might.

Just as he and his train issued from the court-

yard, a troop of gipsies met them. These gipsies
were a queer uncanny folk, whom the speaker describes in rough, vigorous words :—

Now, in your land, gipsies reach you, only
After reaching all lands beside ;
North they go, south they go, trooping or lonely,
And still, as they travel far and wide,
Catch they and keep now a trace here, a trace there,
That puts you in mind of a place here, a place there.
But with us I believe they rise out of the ground,
And nowhere else, I take it, are found
With the earth-tint yet so freshly embrowned ;
Born, no doubt, like insects which breed on
The very fruit they are meant to feed on.
For the earth—not a use to which they don't turn it,
The ore that grows in the mountain's womb,
Or the sand in the pits like a honey-comb,
They sift and soften it, bake it and burn it—
Whether they weld you, for instance, a snaffle,
With side-bars never a brute can baffle ;
Or a lock that's a puzzle of wards within wards ;
Or, if your colt's forefoot inclines to curve inwards,
Horseshoes they'll hammer which turn on a swivel
And won't allow the hoof to shrivel.
Then they cast bells like the shell of the winkle,
That keep a stout heart in the ram with their tinkle ;
But the sand—they pinch and pound it like otters,
Commend me to gipsy glass-makers and potters !
Glasses they'll blow you, crystal clear,
Where just a faint cloud of rose shall appear,
As if in pure water you dropped and let die
A bruise black-blooded mulberry ;
And that other sort, their crowning pride,
With long white threads distinct inside,

Like the lake-flower's fibrous roots which dangle
Loose such a length and never tangle,
Where the bold sword-lily cuts the clear waters,
And the cup-lily couches with all the white daughters ;
Such are the works they put their hand to,
And the uses they turn and twist iron and sand to.

The oldest of the gipsies, a hideous woman, bent double, dressed in ragged wolfskin, and with no eyes at all to speak of, came up to the Duke and offered a present ; for the gipsies come yearly to this Northland, and regularly give their presents to the dukes, always getting a money equivalent.

But this Duke, being of a stingy turn, or having no precedents for gipsies in his books, was not ready for the emergency, and declined to give the old crone anything. So she, to quicken his wits, said she was come to pay her duty to the new young Duchess. This woke the Duke up in another way. He thought what a capital school-mistress this horrible hairy old woman would make for his smooth, delicate girl-wife.

So, briefly telling the old gipsy the story of his wife's wickedness, and commanding her to frighten the lady thoroughly, he ordered the man who tells the story to take the gipsy, and present her to the Duchess.

The man took the gipsy, and bade her follow ; and no sooner had the Duke and his train left, than a marvellous transformation took place in her. She grew taller by a head, and more dignified, and all her aged look vanished ; her old tattered wolfskin changed to a robe fringed with gold coins, and her eyes came out unmistakably.

When the pair arrived at the presence-chamber door, the crone was admitted by the Duchess's tirewoman, Jacynth, who happened also to be the speaker's sweetheart. Jacynth and the gipsy went in, and left the man alone in the balcony. Suddenly he heard a strange melodious sound in the presence chamber; and pushing the window open, he looked in and saw Jacynth lying asleep before the door, and a shape, a queen, that had been the gipsy woman, sitting on the state throne, with the Duchess at her feet. She was speaking or singing to the Duchess in a strange inexpressible melody, which, as the man listened, shaped itself into burning words, telling how life is made for us that we may exercise love on all men and all things throughout the whole world : how that is what the gipsies live to do; and how the Duchess herself may live to do it too, if she will fly from this intolerable splendour and display, become one of the gipsies, and be ever cherished and watched over by them :—

Only, be sure thy daily life,
In its peace, or in its strife,
Never shall be unobserved ;
We pursue thy whole career,
And hope for it, or doubt, or fear,—
Lo, hast thou kept thy path or swerved,
We are beside thee, in all thy ways,
With our blame, with our praise,
Our shame to feel, our pride to show,
Glad, angry—but indifferent, no !
Whether it is thy lot to go,
For the good of us all, where the haters meet,
In the crowded city's horrible street;
Or thou step alone through the morass
Where never sound yet was,
Save the dry quick clap of the stork's bill,
For the air is still, and the water still,
When the blue breast of the dipping coot
Dives under, and all is mute.
So at the last shall come old age,
Decrepit as befits that stage ;
How else wouldst thou retire apart
With the hoarded memories of thy heart,
And gather all to the very least
Of the fragments of life's earlier feast,
Let fall through eagerness to find
The crowning dainties yet behind ?
Ponder on the entire past
Laid together thus at last,
When the twilight helps to fuse
The first fresh, with the faded hues,
And the outline of the whole,
As round eve's shades their framework roll,
Grandly fronts for once thy soul.
And then as, 'mid the dark, a gleam

> Of yet another morning breaks,
> And like the hand which ends a dream,
> Death, with the might of his sunbeam
> Touches the flesh and the soul awakes,
> Then ——

The words stopped. The poor huntsman became suddenly aware that the Duchess was being bewitched. He sprang from the balcony to the ground, and was just going to burst open the door to save her, as he thought, when the Duchess met him, with a face so changed to the beauty of a new-tasted happiness, that he felt all was for the best. So he saddled for her the very palfrey which brought her to the castle to be married, lifted her on it, stammering a few words of clumsy faithfulness, and

> Then, do you know, her face looked down on me
> With a look that placed a crown on me,
> And she felt in her bosom—mark, her bosom—
> And, as a flower-tree drops its blossom,
> Dropped me—ah, had it been a purse
> Of silver, my friend, or gold that's worse,
> Why, you see, so soon as I found myself
> So understood,—that a true heart so may gain
> Such a reward,—I should have gone home again,
> Kissed Jacynth, and soberly drowned myself!
> It was a little plait of hair
> Such as friends in a convent make
> To wear, each for the other's sake,—
> This, see, which at my breast I wear,
> Ever did (rather to Jacynth's grudgment),
> And ever shall, till the Day of Judgment.

And then,—and then,—to cut short,—this is idle,
These are feelings it is not good to foster,—
I pushed the gate wide, she shook the bridle,
And the palfrey bounded,—and so we lost her.

Such is the story ;—a story so simple, now it is
told, that I must crave the indulgence of the philo-
sophic reader who may perchance hope to find
some attempt at profound thought in every line of
these Essays. And what is the moral of the story?
This, too, is so simple that it may seem almost a
platitude. But if I may venture to ask that these
Essays shall be read to the end, it will be seen that
the moral or thought of this poem, simple though
it be, has its place in a scheme, and is but a guide
to deeper speculations to come, as the transparent
brook is our guide to the sea.

Let me be forgiven, then, if I proceed, in homely
phrase, to set forth what seems to be the use and
purpose of this poem, as one in its place in a series.

In this age when, notwithstanding our profes-
sions, we are so apt to think that all the higher
attributes of our common humanity are not common after all, but are confined to the men and
women who lead lives of grace and culture, one
feels thankful to a true poet who is not ashamed
to show us, in uncouth language, the love that can
spring straight from the heart-fountain of rough

servants and immoral vagrants, who through long
unlovely lives have ever striven, without knowing
it, after kindliness and honesty.

What a pathos, fit to draw tears, is there in this
rude simple tale of the poor huntsman! I protest
there are passages in it—which speak of the dumb
striving of a humanity prisoned in too earthy a
chamber, of a yearning which ever and anon, at
the real moments of life, breaks forth in spite of
hindrances — passages, I say, which, while they
move my heart and make my throat swell time
after time, seem always fresh and new as the
spring buds are. The strange awkward attempts at
giving a connected artistic finish to the story; the
light-hearted way in which the man puts down
sentimental fancies (as he would call them) that will
spring up; and the genuine outspoken contempt
for display and nonsense of all kinds—these things,
so truly written down, give to the poem a flavour
which is lacking in smoother compositions, perhaps
more melodious according to the rules of art.

Melody, in its widest sense, is the expression in
any manner howsoever of the love and sympathy of
man for men; and that is the melody which thrilled
the heart of the great man who told this story,
and found an answering chord in the great heart of
the poet who, hearing this story in some far-away

village, **or** reading it in some book of forgotten
folk-lore, knew a loving nature when **he** found **it,**
in whatever **station, in** whatever **age.**

What of this Duchess and her stupid Duke in
their bygone half-barbaric splendour? What of
that old worn-out gipsy in her poverty-stricken
dotage?

As surely as there is a law (which in spoken
words and great men's hearts is centuries old), that
commands us all to give out our hearts in genuine
love and sympathy for all fellow-creatures **with**
whom our lot is cast,—so surely have the Duke
and his mother to answer for their persistent crushing of the hidden love which throbbed beneath the
bosom of the poor little convent girl.

Every man who will not open his heart to the
unspoken desires of a brother for reciprocating love
is sinning not only against himself but against his
whole race, past, present, **and** to come. No man
can say how tremendous may be the effect of
damming up one such love-stream; the swelling
volume of the water will surely at last grow to a
muddy turbulent river, overleap its banks, and
bring devastation and ruin on the fair fields which
bloomed on either side. How often does continual
misunderstanding, caused by coldness which the
smallest effort of will might have dispelled, freeze

into hatred not only of one man or class, but even
of a nation? The terrible consequences tell their
own tale.

But let us turn from the dark side of the picture
to the light thrown on the gipsy crone. Throughout the world, God, who is above human laws and
reverences them not, works with means which men
would despise. What to Him are the virtues
which we call morality and respectability? Nothing.
But love, helpfulness, honesty, are precious as fine
gold.

That old gipsy, so decrepit and doting, was but
the earthen vessel in which, hidden from sight, a
queen soul shone, instinct with power and sympathy.
A soul which, having grown and drawn nourishment
out of the long experience of a hardly-won life,
had learned, straight from God's mouth, lessons
which kings and priests strive and fail to find. She
had gone straight to her great mother, the wife of
God, whom we call Nature; and from her breast
had drawn the yearning which Nature draws from
the divine embrace and sends out in renewed love
for her children and her Husband. From Nature's
touch the old gipsy drew her passion to reclaim
one soul fast slipping into the abyss of indifferentism
and despair From Nature's touch, she who seemed
to the world, perhaps to her own tribe, despicable

and useless, could perpetually renew her life when any struggle to save one human creature demanded her energy. Holding **Nature's hand** she would go right **on until her** body, **worn into** shadow and nothingness, slipped from the arms of her weeping tribe, and her soul flew straight upwards— **whither?**

This is **an old** burden: the poem does but tell us **that it is for love we** are here; not for the love **of a** man for a woman, not for **the love of** a woman **for a man**—not for these only—but for the love of all men and women who seem unlovely, and careworn, and prosaic, whose eyes and **mouths are** depressed with low cares, who have never spoken, **and perhaps** scarcely know **if** they ever thought, what the finely-balanced so-called sympathetic man calls 'beautiful ideas.' The poem is one more voice in **the** multitude of voices which are always crying **to us,** these men and women have in them, though they know **it not,** all the capability, in greater or **less** degree, **of** expressing love if there be need for it, perhaps **not** here, perhaps not even **in the next** life to this, but **at any rate in** God's good time. **Is** it for **us to** slight them **or** speak **harshly of** them? **For** aught we know, any poor **man or woman** may **hold a** fund **of** power **and** sympathy as large, as life-giving **as the** gipsy mother **held;** at least they are all God's as we are, and shall be, as we hope to be, purified and made clean.

Why has this gospel been preached more or less earnestly in all religions, up to the highest of all which the Nazarene burned himself out in proclaiming? Why do we all feel that religion still working within us? Why has the yet higher religion of Positivism based itself on the same sure foundation?

Because, whether in personal or subjective immortality; whether as kings and melodists in a world where there is no night, or scattered among the tribes in inconceivable atoms, our power is never lost; because even as we strive to make perfect our faculty of love here, even to that degree shall we have the boundless delight of its eternal exercise, for healing and helping all who suffer in this earth or in other worlds, when the dress of our flesh has dropped into ashes, and we wake up naked and not ashamed in the unblinding splendour of the life everlasting.

WARING.

IT may seem a paradoxical thing to say, but it is nevertheless true, that all the greatest works of a poet, in the sense of those which have the greatest influence over the thoughts and acts of men, are the works which are most incomplete. Such poems as contain in themselves the complete story or thought which was their life spring (and which are in themselves useful as direct teachings from the master mind in either love, beauty, or knowledge,) have the merit according to their excellence of lessons to the reader, but they are nothing more. The reader sits in the attitude simply of a listener, a pupil, who takes the thing presented and admires it, and sees it in its completeness, but finds no imperative occasion for use of his own thinking powers further than is necessary to the understanding of the actual poem. He is not compelled to pursue any train of thought of his own. But the incomplete works, those which show that the poet's mind worked silently up to the point when he could hold his peace no longer, give a far more serious impetus to the thinking powers of the reader. He feels that a substratum of thought lies beneath, supporting the rough pregnant utterances ; that a long train of reflection must have been pursued before the actual words were written down—a train of reflection which he is piqued into finding out for himself by the very incompleteness of the work before him. He feels that the poem is the birth of the poet's long travail, the very topmost keystone of the arch which he had been building, as it were in secret ; nay, that he himself may, by successful interpretation, become in some sense a discoverer. So much for the use of incomplete poems to each individual reader. But in their collective influence, that is, their influence over minds as a whole, they have a higher use still. All words actually spoken will bear different senses to different minds ; the premises to be assigned to or the conclusions to be drawn from words which, as is the case with these incomplete poems, are only a context, so to speak, of the whole passage or subject which occupied the poet, admit of and will actually meet with far wider differences of interpretation from different minds than completed works do, simply because there is wider range for the exercise of the individuality of each interpreter.

And any true poet would surely rather that his work, whether complete or incomplete in actual words, should furnish a field for the labour of many minds and for much speculation, than that all minds should come to exactly the same conclusion with regard to it. Anything in the world which can exercise men's thinking power, and thereby make them act, must be of use ; and so long as the speculations pursued with regard to these incomplete poems are truthfully pursued, their absolute correctness with regard to the actual thoughts in the poet's mind when he wrote the poem, is a matter of comparatively small importance. If one may venture to carry out these thoughts in a simile, these incomplete poems, already compared to the keystone of an arch, have as a support, not only the first wing of that arch, springing from its first stone, from the first beginnings of the thought thus traced in the poet's brain to fulfilment, but also the other wing of the arch, which, to our eyes, led up to the keystone, seems thrown out downwards from it. From the actual spoken words of the poem, the eyes of the earnest thinker are led downward through the far future, stone by stone, of the thought which thus stands as the thing shown ; his eyes sees new stones, new reflections, new aspirations, all of which will go on adding

G

strength to the fabric, all tending backwards and
upwards to the keystone, till he comes to the last
stone of the arch, the last foundation block which
makes the arch a complete rainbow thing, the final
evolution of the thought or idea at its farthest
bound. But if there be any truth in this simile
of the arch, may we not pursue it a step farther?
In the beginning and ending of the idea which
prompted and is prompted by the poem, there is a
likeness, an equal level, without which the spoken
word, the keystone, cannot be sustained. Whether
it be a life, a death, or a nation's career, of which
the poet tells us, or of which he has been dreaming, all his thought, all our speculations thereon,
spring from that great whole, the world or universe
which is the flooring of the arch. From the world
of men and women, the world of beauty and
warmth, the idea sprang; it ascended hidden in
mists, hidden in the secret places of the poet's
brain; it broke forth in a flame at the highest
point; and once more hidden, when its work of
showing is done, back to the world it returns, for
love of that foundation from which it sprang, to
base itself firm through eternal ages. As the
rainbow's colours are hid in clouds and mist, its
beauties are hid in the brain of the maker; but as
the sun shining on the clouds draws out the colour

of the rainbow, so the warm loving thought of
other minds draws from the hidden place of the
maker's brain the beauties of the thought which is
inclosed there. And suppose that a man sees a
glorious flower hanging high in a forest of verdure,
but can see no path by which he may reach it, is
he not likely to be bettered in craft, in strength, in
the sights he may see, the lessons he may learn, if
he is obliged to find out a path to it, and perchance to climb on hands and knees, and suffer
much hardship to gain it? Does not that man,
having found the flower, gain not only the experience of his journey, but also all the beauties and
fruits which hung around him? Does he not, having
reached the summit where the flower hangs, find a
pleasure, a new knowledge, in going down by a different path with the flower in his hand, keeping its
savour and beauty to cheer him, and still gaining
new growths, new fruits, new knowledge, until he
reaches the kind earth whence sprang both the
upward and the downward path? Even so, a man
trying to trace a path up to the spoken thought,
gains fruits of knowledge, thought, and love, perhaps his own and the poet's, perhaps only his own,
until he arrives at the point when the thought
burst into flower of speech; even so, when he has
reached the spoken thought, he will be bettered by

using his gained experience in treading the path
which still has to be trodden by him; he will be
able to trace new developments in the future of
the thought, by reason of and born of the ideas
which led up to it; he will gain a prophetic power,
a foresight, a use for his own life for the years to
come. Again, we all know how dear both to the
painter and to ourselves are those sudden sketches
in which one piece of colour or form is predomi-
nant, and the rest mere points and lines leading up
to it as to a centre. That sketch is the seizing of
one beauty which mother Nature shows only to her
beloved ones the artists; and it is they only who, as
the priests of Nature, can teach us what is good and
what is not good to be seen in her. The incomplete lines in that sketch show us what in the scene
depicted is, as compared with the completed colour
or form, of minor importance; the painter, who
alone knew their relative value, shows us that we,
the learners, must use his mere rude indications in
order that we may gain to ourselves much force of
imagination by trying to find out what were the
colours, what were the completed forms which in
the original scene filled up those rudimentary lines.
Thus we, the learners, gain a far more vivid idea of
the picture as it was given by nature, than if we

had blindly trusted to a complete picture, satisfying us in all details.

Thus, then, the very reason that the poem of
'Waring' is an incomplete rude sketch, dashed
off by a master who never works carelessly or
without a purpose, would make it worth earnest
study. That it has been chosen as one of the
most important of the Romances, is due, however,
not only to this incompleteness, but also to its
subject, which establishes a yet stronger claim to
consideration and thought. For it deals with the
modern life which is growing up in our midst,
underneath our respectability; the life which, as
one often hears said, has in it far more tragic force
of intellect, fiercer lights and gloomier shades, than
the older times which have become historical.

We are strongly reminded, on reading 'Waring,'
of the obvious truth that the world is very full just
now; that the struggle for life, the perpetual
battle of brain with brain, as it rages at present, is
fiercer and more deadly from day to day. The
actors in this romance enlist our sympathy, because
we feel that its passion belongs so especially to our
own time; because we feel that its incidents in any
other age, when there was less jostling and crowding, could not have taken place at all. And since
every one of the crowd of men perpetually coming

into the world, adds his strength to swell the strife which roars all round us; since the added numbers are daily producing new growths of brain, new thoughts, new actions; the value of the romance is increased by the grandeur of the portrait it draws of one great life, which, though nameless in history, has in its component parts, whether it be a fiction or a reality, many representatives as obscure as Waring; the life of every one of whom is inexpressibly important in the aggregate life of to-day and to-morrow down to future years.

Thus, then, reasons are obvious why it has seemed good to deal with this poem elaborately, not only in the direct thoughts contained in the words of it, but in all the collateral and indirect ideas which a man may by earnest thought create or evolve out of it.

The tale is a simple one. A man, young in years, and whose manners had the reserve of intense pride, used to live in London, unknown save to a score of friends. Even by these, his mighty aspirations occasionally spoken, his astounding claims, rarely put forth, were generally treated as mere wind and vapour. They thought him a dreamer, who was likely to produce no good seed or useful work. But his good-nature seemed so imperturbable that these friends did not hesitate to speak or hint to him their low opinion of his

powers, or at any rate of his achievements. This
sort of thing had gone on for some time, when one
night he disappeared. When they had lost him,
his friends, or at any rate one of them, found out
how much indeed they had loved him ; found out
how much there was in him to love, cherish, revere.
Various guesses were hazarded as to his where-
abouts, his possible future career ; and those who
before had so consistently underrated him, now
prophesied for him all manner of splendid success.
Will he suddenly appear with European fame at
Moscow, a general in the army of the Czar ? Will
he be known as a fiery regenerator of India, or of
forgotten slothful Spain ? Best of all, perhaps he
is hidden somewhere in London,

> And now works on without a wink
> Of sleep, and we are on the brink
> Of something great in fresco paint.
> Some garret's ceiling, walls, and floor,
> Up and down, and o'er and o'er,
> He splashes, as none splashed before
> Since great Caldara Polidore.
> Or Music means this land of ours
> Some favour yet, to pity won
> By Purcell from his rosy bowers—
> ' Give me my so long promised son ;
> Let Waring end what I begun !'
> Then down he creeps and out he steals
> Only when the night conceals
> His face : in Kent 'tis cherry time,
> Or hops are picking : or at prime

Of March he wanders, as, too happy,
Years ago when he was young,
Some mild eve, when woods grew sappy
And the early moths had sprung
To life from many a trembling sheath,
Woven the warm boughs beneath ;
While small birds said to themselves
What would soon be actual song ;
And young gnats, by tens and twelves,
Made as if they were the throng
That crowd around and carry aloft
The sound they have nursed, so sweet and pure,
Out of a myriad noises soft
Into a tone that can endure
Amid the noise of a July noon,
When all God's creatures crave their boon,
All at once and all in tune,
And get it, happy as Waring then,
Having first within his ken
What a man might do with men ;
And far too glad, in the evenglow,
To mix with the world he meant to take
Into his hand, he told you, so,
And out of it his world to make,
To contract or to expand
As he shut or oped his hand.

Will he astonish the world as an actor, a satirist,
a poet, or a dramatist ? How will this strange forgotten star rise again in the heavens that are
yearning for him ?

When all conjectures had proved fruitless and
his friends despaired of ever seeing or hearing of

Waring again, suddenly a man arrived from a cruise
in the Mediterranean, who had seen him—seen him,
not as statesman, artist, or soldier; not in wealth,
luxury, and power; but as a poor sailor, the captain
of a smuggling vessel in Trieste bay.

Such is the story, worked out with much simplicity and grace of diction. Of Waring's character
some especially vivid passages give us a speaking
portrait. With an almost feminine softness of character, he blended a sternness which was forgotten
in presence of his ever ready sympathy and good-
nature. His love, offered willingly to but rejected
by his friends, is compared to the gracious love of
some lady with a tender but unbeautiful face, who
in years gone by had with untiring patience made
gentle but unsuccessful attempts to gain a nestling-
place in the flinty bosoms of intellectual male
youths, imperially arrogant. She, ever patient,
ever tender, would not reproach, but, like Waring,
when, all too late, they thrust from them her full
bounty of nature, retired without a murmur, looking back with sad wistful eyes on the blind fools
who knew not that they were slighting and despising an angel.

> E'en so, swimmingly appears,
> Through one's after-supper musings,
> Some lost lady of old years

With her beauteous vain endeavour
And goodness unrepaid as ever ;
The face, accustomed to refusings,
We, puppies that we were . . . Oh never,
Surely, nice of conscience, scrupled
Being aught like false, forsooth, to?
Telling aught but honest truth to?
What a sin, had we centupled
Its possessor's grace and sweetness !
No ! she heard in its completeness
Truth, for truth's a weighty matter,
And truth at issue, we can't flatter !
Well, 'tis done with ; she's exempt
From damning us thro' such a sally ;
And so she glides, as down a valley,
Taking up with her contempt,
Past our reach ; and in, the flowers
Shut her unregarded hours.

The closing scene, showing the sternness of
Waring's nature, as indicated by the pitiless contempt with which he had left his friends without a
word of leavetaking, is worth study.   'When I last
saw Waring,' says his friend,

We were sailing by Trieste,
Where a day or two we harboured ;
A sunset was in the west,
When, looking over the vessel's side,
One of our company espied
A sudden speck to larboard ;
And as a sea-duck flies and swims
At once, so came the light craft up,
With its sole lateen sail, that trims

And turns (the water round its rims
Dancing, as round a sinking cup,)
And by us like a fish it curled,
And drew itself up close beside,
Its great sail on the instant furled,
And o'er its planks a shrill voice cried
(A neck as bronzed as a Lascar's),
' Buy wine of us, you English brig ?
Or fruit, tobacco and cigars ?
A pilot for you to Trieste ?
Without one, look you ne'er so big,
They'll never let you up the bay !
We natives should know best.'
I turned, and ' Just those fellows' way,'
Our captain said.   ' The 'long-shore thieves
Are laughing at us in their sleeves.'

In truth, the boy leaned laughing back,
And one, half-hidden, by his side,
Under the furled sail, soon I spied,
With great grass hat and kerchief black,
Who looked up with his kingly throat,
Said somewhat, while the other shook
His hair back from his eyes, to look
Their longest at us.'

This closing scene contains analogies which cannot be passed over in silence. At sunset of the
day—sunset of Waring's life in England—he, like
the sun about to disappear, shone forth once more
before he sank beneath the intellectual horizon of
his friends. At the moment when it seemed there
was no hope in England of hearing more of him,

his little frail smuggling craft came dancing up by
the big formidable English vessel in which his
friend was sailing, and offered to bargain with
them and help them.   These confident British
youths were just becoming aware that it was possible their sun might set and leave them dark,
when he shone out once more; but not to give
them light: the time was past for that.   They in
their former arrogance, symbolised by the English
brig, had disdained Waring, in his shyness, reserve,
and incapacity, symbolised by the seemingly in-
capable smuggling smack, just as the brig, with its
captain and its crew, disdained the help of the
smuggler.   Waring left his friends when they refused to acknowledge him: the smuggler left the
brig when she disdained his offers.   The English-
men were left to look big and try and shoulder
through the world: the brig was left to try and
get up Trieste bay; both without Waring for a
pilot.   Even as the smuggling craft went off into
the rosy and golden sunset to begin a new day,
leaving the brig in a hopeless night behind it,
pilotless, so did Waring, to begin his new day,
leave his ungrateful friends in the night of their
stupidity and ignorance.

'Then the boat,
I know not how, turned sharply round,

Laying her whole side on the sea
As a leaping fish does ; from the lee
Into the weather, cut somehow
Her sparkling path beneath our bow ;
And then went off, as with a bound,
Into the rosy and golden half
Of the sky, to overtake the sun
And reach the shore, like the sea-calf
Its singing cave ; yet I caught one
Glance ere away the boat quite passed—
And neither time nor toil could mar
Those features : so 1 saw the last
Of Waring !' You? Oh, never star
Was lost here, but it rose afar !
Look east, where whole new thousands are !
In Vishnu-land what Avatar ?

Such are the main features which strike us in the spoken words of the poem. It is but a sketch, and no more ; a few powerful lines giving a vivid portrait ; a bit of central drawing, with the accessories of past and future only hinted. These hints, and the incompleteness of the sketch, tempt us to indulge in a world of speculation on the past of Waring's life, before and up to the period of his disappearance ; and on the future of his life, after his reappearance, to the end.

How had this wondrous nature first sprung up from the great level plain of humanity, to culminate in the crisis which gives occasion for the poem ? How did his soul rise to the topmost keystone of

the arch, that highest act of intellectual daring, the
knowledge when to separate himself from his friends,
break off ruthlessly all old and dear ties, and begin
a new life? To learn this, let us trace his life from
its beginning to that point when he so dared and
achieved.

Nursed in luxury, brought up as a gentleman in
the conventional sense, did he not weary of a round
of colourless days, chafe at perpetual petty observances? In his youth he had wandered up and
down—a solitary *gauche* youth, mingling with his
mother Nature, and dreaming of what he would do
with the world. He was not a man who had been
soured and warped by poverty; he must have been
well to do, for we find his friends blaming him for
not writing and speaking earlier—blaming him for
laziness and pride, for voluntarily choosing not to
mix with the world.

Slighted from his earliest boyhood, he very early
cast aside what he called the trammels of conventionality; wandering whither he would, he soon
overcame or silenced the remonstrances of a fond
mother—of aunts or sisters who found him incorri-
gible, nay, most likely saw nothing in him except a
very awkward creature, perpetually in everybody's
way. Awkward enough, possibly; but tall and
straight, with large eyes, often dull in expression,

only lighting up **by fits**; a colourless, almost lifeless face, with **no** feature **to recommend it, save a brow** preternaturally broad **and** full, a mouth wide, firm set, and tender, given rarely to twitching, **of** kinship with the eyes, but trenched **on** either side by early pronounced lines from the far-stretching **nostril**— lines that gave a settled look of scorn **to the face** behind which so much **love** lay hid. A **face** which looked at you without any consciousness of expres- sion in it, without trying **to see what** effect he **was** producing, only seeming to know **that** you were a human being who must be loved if possible, and whose aspirations, if you would but give them, should meet with a full response and **a warm embrace!**

Early in **his** life he thought he saw **all** that was wrong in the world; with the confidence **of** youth, day by day he would strike **out, in** his woodland walks, utopian plans, whereby perhaps artists should be made rich and appreciated (for he must have had an artist's nature), armies should be **reor-** ganised, monarchies overthrown, the poor made well off, republics raised into being, education en- forced, game laws, excise laws, monopolies, sunk in an ocean of freedom. For this young fighter, un- worn **as yet by** actual struggle with men and **women,** was superb in his self-created supremacy.

But at last a time came when he must leave his

loneliness and mix with the crowd of London.
How would he behave there? He feels too certain
of his own originality of conception to desire a large
circle of friends ; he is too proud and impatient
of falseness to gain himself a place and a name by
flattery or acknowledgment of famous charlatans,
almost too proud to give praise even to famous
true men.

With a spirit truly regal, for it trusted in its own
power above all else, he was content to let friends
come to him, without caring to seek them. But in
his intercourse with men of his own age he con-
tracted a few friendships which he maintained with
strict loyalty. To these he gave all his inmost
soul; to them he told all his plans, all his aspirations. But alas, his confidence only met with good-
natured rebuffs; for his friends were still tied and
bound, as Waring would have said, with the chain
of precedent and public opinion, and dared not call
those men obscure whom the world called famous,
dared not recognise one whom the world had not
yet recognised : and what was he, who, save
scribbling a few rough notes, had done nothing
to reveal his inner nature, that he should claim
for himself a place above all the great men of
the day? But the blows so good-naturedly dealt
him by his friends only seemed to make him

tougher: day by day his strong will and ever
youthful individuality sprang up fresher from renewed rebuffs, and his intellect grew until a fixed
purpose had formed itself. Hitherto he had done
nothing but dream and talk ; try as he would, he
could not make men acknowledge his self-known
worth, and still less as it seemed could he by mere
talk and jottings of ideas make his plans known to
the world. How was he to do this? If he went on
dreaming, he must at last sink into a discontented
railer; he must indeed acknowledge that these
well-meaning friends were right and the world
better as it was. Gradually he came to see that he
must do some *actual* thing before he could hope
to assert his place in the world.

At the very time when the blows seemed to rain
thickest, when his spirit seemed most beaten, his
inner nature was arming him for a last struggle.

In silence he laid his plans for intellectual escape,
but it was to be an escape from bondage to freedom, from the kingship of dreams to the empire of
fact. How was he to begin? Seeing how useless
his dreaming life had been, his thoughts naturally
turned in the opposite direction, towards a life
which would admit of no dreaming.

To bid farewell for a time to all imperial visions,
to quench his love of abstractions and deal with

hard actual facts, was no light thing; but to go
away from the intellectual life which had been so
dear, so barren of fruit, and learn new lessons from
the physical life, was very hard.   And yet the
thing must be done; he had laid down the principle
that no man can prove himself unless he has the
energy to develope his body; and now was the
time to try how that principle worked.   In what
way would he arrange his plans for the first step
towards physical development?   To enlist in the
army in London or enter the navy, would be to
ensure himself a brute's life for years, and the even-
tual discovery some day that his intellect was dead
indeed.   No; whatever the service, it must at least
fulfil the condition of giving not only freedom from
brutality in its associations, but, if possible, brainwork, though of the lowest sort; it must also chime
in with his pre-established sympathies, which rather
rebelled against established forms of government.

But in laying his plans for this new life, in which
he was to be born again as a babe just awaking in
a new world, one important detail did not escape
his attention.   Hitherto his greatest dreams had
been of power; power was the god of his worship,
or rather was the hidden jewel which he strove to
find and keep.   In that placid brow and undemon-
strative mouth were lines which indicated a terrible

force lurking within, hitherto **kept** under by **per-petual reverses,** but nourishing **its** strength **all** the same; hitherto kept quiet **by the** caressing sympathy of his nature, but ready, **when** occasion should call **for it,** to leap **forth and** assert **its** existence unmistakably.

Thus, while considering how **to** train his body, **he** did **not** forget the importance of that **desire to** dominate. Some time **he meant to use it with a** purpose; **to take** the world ' **into his** hand, **he told** you, so !' **and in** order to fit himself for that consummation he must now **choose** some bodily employment which gave him captainship.

Dismissing the **idea** of serving **as a** soldier **or** sailor for England, **he** glanced for **a** moment **at** continental armies. But **then,** service **in** them would involve **too** much attention **to** drill, **too** much martinet discipline, to suit Waring's hitherto **loose and** ungoverned notions; besides which **he** could scarcely become a soldier at all in Europe (unless **he went to** the Polish patriots) **without** serving the cause of one who, in **his eyes,** was a despot. **Spain** was **too sunk in sloth** and immorality; **he** was not **ready yet to** regenerate Turkey, whatever dreams he **might** have ; in Sweden and Norway the **men** were too content : **so that** soldiership **in** Europe seemed a useless

career, unless he could work for some cause of
freedom. Was it the word ' freedom' that suggested
to him Italy? Italy! Was not hers a cause of
freedom? But when he came to consider it
fairly, his mind, hitherto undisciplined, grew impatient at the thought of the useless embroilment
of a political warfare, such as the cause of Italy
would, in his own judgment, involve; besides
which, the first step of heading a band of Patriots
seemed distasteful to him when he recollected
all that he had heard of Italian soldiery; and he
shrank from the name of banditti. Perhaps, too,
he felt himself too untutored at present, and
mistrusted his capability to undertake a cause
which, as he believed, must, unless thoroughly ably
handled, involve much sin and little good. He
was going to begin a new life in an elementary
state of being; what he wanted then was some
simple elemental physical life, some simple elemental physical command; a life and a post which,
while leaving large room for contemplation, would
afford not only opportunities for stern action, exercise of courage, nerve, and generalship, but also
continual contact with and influence over a few
simple men, unknowing of much evil, unscathed by
the strong hand of despotism.

Thwarted in every direction on land, his thoughts

turned to the sea; and since no field for his labour was at present discernible out of Europe, the Mediterranean must be his training-ground.

He remembered how in former cruises he had seen smuggling craft, with wine, fruit, tobacco—all kinds of contraband goods—going up and down like sea-fowl, rarely harmed, because apparently so inoffensive.

Musing on these, he began to draw a parallel between their physical and his own intellectual life. They had found the physical laws of society too hard and binding: he had found the intellectual laws the same. They had been always treated as low despicable folk, with no good in them; so had he. They had rebelled against men's contempt or repulsion and sought a life for themselves, as he was going to do. They were free, as he hoped to be. Waring, the self-constituted intellectual king of the world, dethroned by those subjects who would never acknowledge his sway, takes the crown from his brow and goes forth;—not to seek fellowship with the prosperous and wealthy, not to commune with other intellects in other lands, but to find brotherhood with the lowest, simplest men, among whom at least he could learn how to love unchecked, and who at least would return his love.

In their company he could learn what the winds

and waters sang ; why the sunset yearned, the sun-
rise aspired. They would teach him how to bear
and be strong; and while they helped him in
hospitable offices, he could show them new paths,
new hopes, new aims.

Thus, joining sympathy with the lowest to aims
after the highest life, and both these to direct
bodily culture, he embarked in the opportunity thus
afforded for developing old dreams all his capital
of energy, and deserved to succeed.

His sun has set in England, the ship of his life
has sailed beyond the extreme sea-line ; the star of
Waring will be seen no more in English skies.
But there are other heavens !

In Vishnu land what Avatar ?

Look at him gradually stealing his way into the
hearts of his sailors, until they change from wild
simple loving men, to instructed cultivated thrifty
seamen, with hopes beyond plunder, fears beyond
priesthood, and desires for better things than a
wild sea life and occasional debauches. Is this
Waring the dreamer ? This man who, firm-sinewed
and healthy of brain, is brother and captain to
these poor contrabandists ? He and they have
done for each other the utmost they could do in
this poor earth; but he has bade them a passionate

farewell for a new work, and a new life. Like lovers he and they have been. Have they not sung songs and prayed prayers beneath the yearning sky, in front of the unknown sunsets? Have they not given healing and help to all who needed it, man, woman, and child? Waring, in his sailors' eyes, is godlike : they think he holds in his bosom secrets of heaven and earth. The fame of his craft, courage, and strength will ring down the shores of the Mediterranean for many years, when he has passed away. Is this Waring the dreamer?

But there is work to be done yet; and his strong individual nature and a kind of selfishness in him demand work which gives fruition. Seeing as he does, that any attempt at regeneration in Europe must eventuate in failure at first, in a mad striving after impossible ends, and certainly in much bloodshed, remembering that he himself could expect, even if he attempted any such regeneration, no sight of that for which he has toiled, he falls back on that idea of working simple elemental natures which has proved such a success, and determines to apply the same principle in a wider field.

Europe sickens his peculiarly fastidious intellect: there is too much civilisation, too much intrigue, too much hurry, and, as he thinks, too much selfishness. Where in the world are there men who, while

more advanced in intellect than the sailors, have
their grand simplicity, their love and hospitality,
their pure reverence? Not in Europe, nor in Africa,
nor probably in America. But are there no Eastern
races with creeds, philosophers, poets of their own,
scarcely a word of whose wisdom or beauty has
reached these cold regions? What of India? There
England, which has discarded Waring, exercises
what he considers the most gigantic despotism of
the earth; there the European, tyrannising, not over
other Europeans, but over the inferior brain of the
Asiatic, forces him to yield up his rich land to
aggrandise the greatest merchant race in the world.
What war can be holier than a crusade against in-
vaders not only of hearths and homes, but of morals,
religion, intellectual life, and all the inner feelings
of a great but enervated nation?

Here in the East may Waring's star rise, to lead
a new company of wise men to their redemption;
he perchance will be the man who shall bring to
triumphant fulfilment that idea of emancipation of
India from European thraldom which, since Waring
was seen in Trieste bay, has already made itself felt
through the fervid words of a few earnest thinkers.

Now what lessons does the poet intend that we
should learn by this life of Waring, such as it has
been, such as it will be? These lessons seem to be

two : one which concerns Waring's character, the other which concerns the responsibilities of his friends towards him.

In the manner of Waring's development of his own nature, we observe throughout a carelessness of other people's opinion and an apparent selfishness in pursuing his own ends. But when a man has, as Waring seems to have had, certain fixed ideas, no matter what, of whose truth he feels certain, is it not better for him to work them out by himself, to make mistakes it may be, and have to tread over again the old ground, thus losing much time ; is it not better, so soon as he has discovered any one idea which is indubitably his own, that he should carry it out to its furthest consequences, always judging for himself as much, and consulting others as little, as possible ? Is it not better, in short, to keep each man's individuality pure and unsullied, so far as possible ? This world of men, though it be a great whole, is yet made up of men each of whom is a world in himself; each has doubtless the same groundwork of nature, but in the common attributes of each one there are such wide differences in degree as to constitute almost differences in kind. It is by the proper use of these differences of degree that the work of the world is carried on ; and wherever any one natural attribute is so peculiarly developed in a man as to amount almost to an individual quality, it is surely the man's duty to make that attribute do its fullest work by employing it to the utmost, so far as he honestly can. That attribute is a thing with an innate force of its own; it grows with daily exercise; if it receives assistance from other minds it rapidly degenerates in strength, just like a child for ever walking in leading strings; losing its self-supporting power, it does not perform half the work in the world which it would perform if self-nurtured. Let it then be subjected to the rigorous exercise which it will be sure to give itself, if left alone to the man's own self-esteem and the help of his other faculties.

On such grounds as these it was thoroughly right for Waring to dream out his dreams, so long as he kept clearly before him what he was doing; his dreams perpetually led him into mistakes, but those mistakes made him patient, roused his ingenuity, kept his faith in exercise by the perpetual whipping of doubt; and at last drove his soul onward to that step whose wisdom was proved by its issue.

Waring, who was not ashamed to blot out all his past life almost as if it had not been, who did not flinch from learning all his lesson of life afresh like a little child, was a stronger man at the end of the

mental struggle through which he passed to gain
that step than he was at its beginning, just as a
man is stronger at the end than he was at the
beginning of a course of physical training; and the
consequences showed themselves in any influence
for good which he had with the sailors; may show
themselves in future influences for good in India.
Whatever good has been done or shall be done
hereafter will have been accomplished by means of
that stern development of self, as distinguished
from absorption into other minds, which Waring
strove to work out.

But what shall we say of the responsibilities of
his friends? Here were men who, by ordinary insight, might have seen that they had a prince
among them; a rare nature, which, instead of being
crushed and thwarted, should have been gently en-
couraged and soothed; a nature which these common men ought to have been well content only to
have kept alive. But instead of this, they perpetually baffled him by senseless laughter and more
senseless exhortations; and had not the power of
his individuality sustained him, had not his strong
kindly insight into all human nature kept his
temper true, his intellect must have died beneath
their hands. As it was, their punishment was
adequate; for by their blundering they lost, not only

for themselves but for England and for Europe too, a soul which would have shone like a beacon to light all nations.

Every man of us is responsible to himself and to the world for the manner in which he treats the intellect of every companion, be that intellect great or small: how much more then is he responsible, not only to himself and to the world but to that companion, if he fails to do all he can to foster any exceptional powers which may lie hid under an uncongenial surface?

The murder of a man's soul is just as culpable as the murder of his body. The men who would not acknowledge Waring till it was too late were indeed to all intents killers of his soul, although they did not succeed in crushing him; and every man who sins as they sinned will have a bitter reckoning to pay some day, either to himself or the world, when the divinity which might have saved us soars away in sad disgust from an unappreciative humanity.

'BEFORE' AND 'AFTER.'

THESE two poems, in a few lines, place before us
a series of arguments on the duty of men to avenge
wrong. The motive of the poems is a quarrel
which has taken place between two men; and the
arguments used both for and against the prosecu-
tion of the quarrel are vivified, first in the mind of
a bystander, roused by a sense of wrong done
somewhere, second in the mind of the wronged
man, when he has glutted his vengeance.

Few of the author's works, even including his
dramas, display so fully as does the poem called
'Before' the universal existence in mankind, not
only of a natural striving after the truth, but also
of that hatred of tyranny and wrong, high faith,
and stern sense of justice above forgiveness, which
prompt the feeling, very seldom expressed, that we
are here as champions for the right, and cannot
afford to carry out to the utmost Christian prin-
ciples; while in the few lines called 'After,' we
have an equally masterly delineation of the remorse

which attacks a brave kindly man, whose blood, roused a moment ago to madness, has now, after he has wrought his vengeance, sunk to an ebb in solemn repentance.

The scene in 'Before,' shows us two men who have on a sudden determined to refer a deadly quarrel to the ordeal of battle.

The usual peacemaker is there, the usual bellicose second.

But there is also present a man who, perhaps, seeing clearer than either of these what must be the consequences of letting such a quarrel right itself, and in order if possible to get at the truth, puts before the peacemaker a number of arguments, clear, forcible and complete in themselves, though not unanswerable.

Let them fight it out, friend! things have gone too far,
God must judge the couple! leave them as they are:
Whichever one's the guiltless, to his glory,
And whichever one the guilt's with, to my story.

Why, you would not bid men, sunk in such a slough,
Strike no arm out further, stick and stink as now,
Leaving right and wrong to settle the embroilment,
Heaven with snaky hell, in torture and entoilment?

The thought which we may fairly express in prose as that which is the key to the meaning of this poem is as follows:

Here have two men quarrelled, and we do not know which is the wrongdoer, which the wronged man : all we do know is that a wrong has been done.

Both men are eager to fight, urged either by hate, fear of suspense, or desire for vengeance.

This being so, no human judgment can avail to settle the dispute ; for the wrongdoer will not confess, and if he did, the wronged man's blood is so hot, that confession and human penalty will not suffice him. So we must leave them to the impulses which God gave them, impulses whose springs we cannot see, but which God alone can work, and will work to the displaying of the truth. For if the wronged man gets the victory, as he ought to do, his remorse (he being human) will too surely force him into speech which will show clearly that it was the dead (or conquered) man who did the wrong. If the wrongdoer gets the victory, *his* remorse, doubly severe for his first wrong, and the second shame of killing an innocent man, will force the truth from *his* lips.

Thus, in any event, the truth must appear ; and when a wrong has been done, it is better that it should come to the world's sight, even through the death of one man, than that the mystery should remain untold, making a festering sore of lies in the wrongdoer, a festering sore of injury unavenged in the **wronged** man; and leaving **the world** at large in suspense and puzzlement, **to deal** its random blows of judgment and **criticism** against both alike, and through them against àll mankind, who are bound alike in the chain of fellowship, and no one of whom can suffer without affecting the rest.

If we are to leave every entanglement to be unravelled by abstract laws of right and wrong, with no agency of man, we shall find ourselves in a slough of calamity indeed ; the age of miracles is past; God is silent, and has retreated behind a veil of centuries ; he leaves men now to work out the world by themselves, and having so left them, he will never be too hard in judging a little wrong, done to secure a great right, the right of truth.

Thus we have dealt with the wrong done, as it must exist in one of these two men.

Now let us deal with each of the two in turn, and see how they will be better or worse for fighting the quarrel out.

> Who's the culprit of them ?   How must he conceive
> God—the queen he caps to, laughing in his sleeve,
> ' 'Tis but decent to profess oneself beneath her ;
> Still, one must not be too much in earnest, either !'   ·

> Better sin the whole sin, sure that God observes,
> Than go live his life out ! Life will try his nerves,
> When the sky, which noticed all, makes no disclosure,
> And the earth keeps up her terrible composure.

to us a series of pure thoughts, the result of his labour, it is better surely to give our whole mind to developing these thoughts; for in reality any divergence or inquiry into the ways by which those thoughts are produced, the accessories by which they are supported, would be a waste of force. It is the real gold we come to seek: we care nothing for the nature of the clay in which it is imbedded. It is the naked mistress we desire; the how, when, and where of her silk and linen is no affair of ours.

It is now time to take up the story of Sordello, and the construction of the poem, and to give an account, as concise as possible, of the *action* of the poem, treating, so far as it may serve this object, of the history of the principal characters. It is scarcely necessary to say that the whole of this part of the subject is extracted from the poem itself.

Between 600 and 700 years ago Lombardy was split into two factions, called Guelf and Ghibellin. The former, Lombards by birth, were firm allies and subjects of the Pope. The latter, immigrants from Saxon Germany, were feudatories of the Kaiser.

These two great parties were naturally always at feud. In Mantua they were represented by two

families: the Guelf by the Adelardi, the Ghibellin
by the Salinguerra family, who had also large
possessions in Ferrara. The heir of the Adelardi
family at that time was a girl named Linguetta.
The head of the Salinguerra family had just died,
and his heir, Taurello, was under age. A marriage
had been arranged by old Salinguerra between his
son Taurello and Linguetta, which would have
united in his house the wealth and power of the
two factions, and established the supremacy of the
Ghibellins in Mantua. At his death, however, the
Guelfs of Mantua, jealous for their faction, repu-
diated this arrangement, carried off Linguetta, and
married her to Azzo d'Este, Lord of the Guelfs.
Young Taurello, in natural wrath at this treachery,
withdrew from Mantua, nursing in his breast a deep-
rooted hatred of the d'Este family. He made
alliance with Heinrich the Kaiser, whose daughter
Retrude he married. He then returned with tokens
from Heinrich to Mantua, dislodged Azzo from the
Salinguerra palace in Ferrara, and completely over-
bore the Guelf faction in the two cities. The chief
of the Ghibellins, Ecelin Romano, seeing Taurello's
energy of character, invited him to Vicenza, holding
out as an inducement the promise of his aid to
secure Taurello's complete restoration in Mantua
and Ferrara. This plot, however, being detected

by Azzo, and by Richard Boniface, Count of Verona, who were both then in the city, Ecelin and Taurello were expelled. **But** in their **flight they** burned **Vicenza, and** Salinguerra's wife **Retrude** and his **boy were** both reported as killed. Ecelin had had **many** wives: his present wife **was Adelaide** the Tuscan, **a** woman whose indomitable energy and consummate craft kept him in his place as head of the Ghibellins. At the burning of Vicenza **the** panic-stricken Ecelin basely left Adelaide and **her** child to be saved by a common archer, while **her** own and Ecelin's escape from the city was entirely due to Taurello's daring. Adelaide, seeing **at this** juncture that Taurello, **not** Ecelin, was **the real** chieftain, **was moved by** admiration of the one and scorn of the **other** to snatch from the **carnage** Taurello's wife and child, who thus escape**d the** burning. The mother, Retrude, died in the journey. **The** child was Sordello.

Adelaide's motive in saving him appears **to** have been to make him in due time head of the **Ghi-**bellins. He was taken by her to Goito Castle, near Mantua, where she gave it out that he was the child of the archer who had saved her. Her reason **for her** present concealment of **Sordello's** real birth **was, as** I think, that she did not choose to let Ecelin know the truth until Sordello was old

enough to take the station she intended for him;
and it has been suggested to me that her reason
for keeping Taurello in ignorance was that she
saw he would have no care to assert his real place
if he thought he had no son to succeed him, and
that he could thus be kept more securely in the
service of Ecelin. I think this suggestion is
valuable; but that her real motive was a desire
that Taurello's aggrandisement should be wrought
by her hands alone. Before, however, she could
carry out her project for Sordello, she died.

During the infancy and boyhood of Sordello,
Adelaide also brought up at Goito Castle a girl
named Palma, daughter of Ecelin by a former wife.
She was betrothed in early life to young Richard,
Count Boniface. At Goito Castle Sordello lived
in seclusion till he reached the age of eighteen or
twenty, when he visited Mantua, where by a fortunate chance he was enabled to display his gift of
song, to the discomfiture of Eglamor, the Chief
Troubadour of Richard Boniface, at a Love Court
which Richard and Palma were holding there previous to their espousal. This was almost the first
time Palma had seen Sordello, and she fell in deep
love with him. Eglamor died of grief at his defeat,
and Sordello was appointed Palma's minstrel. As
such he lived at Mantua for about ten or twelve

years, getting various meeds of applause and cen-
sure.

After **the** death of Retrude and the **supposed**
death of his child, Taurello seemed to **lose all care**
for chieftainship in Mantua or elsewhere; he there-
fore of his own will put himself second **to** Ecelin,
and became his Prime Minister. In this capacity
he ruled at Ferrara a number of turbulent years
(signalised by perpetual broils between Ghibellin
and Guelf), until, about a year before Sordello's
death, Adelaide died ; and Ecelin, left a prey to **his**
own weak impulses, retired to a convent, gave up
his place as head of Romano, and dismissed Taurello. Taurello, thus deserted, went to **his native**
town Mantua for **a time.** Meanwhile the nego-
tiation for Richard's and Palma's marriage proceeded, and after a short stay at Mantua, Taurello
returned to Ferrara, where the Guelfs since Ecelin's
defection had gained ground. Taurello, seeing
that Romano's fortunes were tottering, and being
desirous at **all** hazards to prevent the total absorption of that house into the Guelf faction, which
would ensue if Palma married Richard, left Ferrara
for Padua, and visited Palma at Goito, gained her
consent to postpone the marriage, and her authority
to **act as** Romano's Vice-regent, rightly judging
that the Ferrarese Guelfs would give him an

occasion to break off the match, by committing
some outrage on the Ghibellins there.   His judgment was right.   The Guelfs took advantage of
his absence to burn and plunder everything Ghibellin.   Then came Taurello and restored order,
crushing the Guelfs.   On this Azzo and Richard
Boniface besieged Ferrara ; and at last Taurello,
calling a parley, induced Richard to enter Ferrara,
and kept him there a prisoner.

Palma this while was in Verona waiting, an un-
willing bride, to be espoused to Richard, who had
by Taurello's adroitness been trapped into breaking
his engagement, and made a prisoner in Ferrara.
Palma, who loved Sordello only, and who knew the
secret of his birth, summoned him from Goito
(whither he had retired after his first failure as a
poet in Mantua) to visit her in Verona.   She told
him how near to destruction Ecelin's defection had
brought Romano's house, and how as the chief of
her house she had authorised Taurello to take
extreme measures for maintaining Romano's as-
cendancy; and being determined to advance Sordello's fortunes and wed him herself, persuaded
him to come with her to Ferrara in disguise, before
the arbitrators could arrive who were to treat for
Count Richard's ransom.   They arrived at Ferrara,
and had audience of Taurello.   The result of the

interview was that Taurello (who had acted on Palma's licence, entertained proposals of the Kaiser, and obtained from him authority to name the head of Romano) invested Sordello with the badge of the house. Within twenty-four hours after he had been invested with this dignity, Sordello died.

As to the construction of the poem, it is in form a narrative; and the poet apologises at the outset for taking the historic mode, instead of making Sordello speak for himself in his own manner. But as the analysis of a soul is his great object, it is surely of the highest importance to give the development of that soul a stamp of portraiture as clear and direct as possible ; to reproduce not only modes of thought, but even as far as possible turns of expression. And while on the one hand it is imperatively necessary for the workman to absorb himself into the subject-matter of his work in such a poem as this, on the other hand the narrative form is by far the most tempting to any display of the author's individuality. Still, although we must lament that all established rules were not thrown away, for the sake of presenting the clear picture with which it is undoubtedly the poet's earnest desire to furnish us, we must not forget that what we lose in the way I have indicated we gain not

only in sympathy with the mind which produces
the work, but also in the good result of such toil as
the added obscurity entails upon us.

As to historical framework, the dedication gives
us to understand that it has no further promin-
ence than a background requires; but is it good
(I ask as one unversed in technical construction)
that the history should be told as it is, backwards?

The opening scene occurs just before Sordello's
death; and when we are already somewhat exhausted with the effort of understanding that opening scene, we are ruthlessly hurried back to the
beginning of the real action of the story, and find
ourselves at a loss to account for dates. Then
again, after bringing us through Sordello's development to the close of his life, that is to the date at
which the opening scene took place, is it fair to
plunge us in a vast sea of digression into Browning's own inner life, occupying nearly four hundred
lines, which comprise perhaps the hardest part of
the book, and utterly throw us out of the unity of
the story?

But it is time to say something of the character
of Sordello.

Roughly, his life may be divided, according to

a hint in the poem, into two portions or circles,
by no means equal in extent of time, but quite
equal in respect of importance. The first three
books are taken up with his development as a
great egoist. The last three books are taken up
with his development as a great altruist ; and in
both circles he ended at the point, and with the
same hopes, from which he started.

> For he—for he,
> Gate-vein of this heart's-blood of Lombardy,
> (If I should falter now)—for he is Thine !
> Sordello, thy forerunner, Florentine !
> A herald-star I know thou didst absorb
> Relentless into the consummate orb
> That scared it from its right to roll along
> A sempiternal path with dance and song
> Fulfilling its allotted period,
> Serenest of the progeny of God,
> Who yet resigns it not ! His darling stoops
> With no quenched lights, desponds with no blank troops
> Of disenfranchised brilliancies, for, blent
> Utterly with thee, its shy element,
> Like thine upburneth prosperous and clear.
> Still, what if I approach the august sphere
> Named now with only one name, disentwine
> That under-current, soft and argentine,
> From its fierce mate in the majestic mass,
> Leavened as the sea whose fire was mixt with glass
> In John's transcendent vision—launch once more
> That lustre? Dante, pacer of the shore
> Where glutted hell disgorgeth filthiest gloom,
> Unbitten by its whirring sulphur-spume—

Or whence the grieved and obscure waters slope
Into a darkness quieted by hope ;
Plucker of amaranths grown beneath God's eye
In gracious twilights where His chosen lie,
I would do this! if I should falter now!

BOOK I.

In dealing with the first circle of his life, we must consider Sordello's development as *man*, and the creation of his poetic soul, by the influence of his commerce with inanimate nature.

He lived in his boyhood at Goito Castle in the enjoyment of childish and boyish pleasures; in the warm weather watching outdoor nature; in the winter peering through the picture galleries and dim chambers. His face, with its wide delicate nostril, sharp cut, restless lips, and calm brow, indicated a soul fit to receive delight at every sense. Framed for pleasure, his was the finer sense for which the skies are bluer, the sun more dazzling, than for other men. Such was Sordello· *in his boyhood.*

Now the souls of poets may be divided into two broad classes. The first is one which, loving every disclosure of Nature in turn for the sake of its beauty, and investing each idol of an hour with life

from his own soul, strives to blend itself with, and
absorb itself irrevocably into, every external fresh
discovered beauty. The second is frequently a
development of, but is always stronger in this life
than, the first, and always overthrows it here when
they come into collision. He looks on external
beauty not as a thing to be worshipped, glorified,
and blended with, but as a revealment of a like
quality preexistent in himself, hitherto hidden or
only dormant; he asserts his power at any instant
by force of his will to rouse into being within
himself the prototype of any form of nature, from
earth's simplest shape to heaven's most complex
essence. But it is sad to find these souls sinking
into indolence, since, as they say, this life, and time,
are too narrow an arena to display their full power
of mastery; and it is still sadder, if a desire seizes
them to force this life, and time, to display their
full power of mastery here, instead of waiting for
the opportunity which only another life, or perhaps
eternity, can afford. Now, whether Sordello's soul
was one of the first or second class described, or a
modification of either or both, it will be the task of
an honest translator of this poem to determine.
His boyhood glided calmly away at Goito Castle,
his only human associates being some old women-
servants. In full health and youth, his imagination

wreathed about each new discovery in the nature round him some infantile conceit, imparting in fancy to each in turn so much of his own thought and sense as he hoped would enable it to stand alone and serve him as a companion, toiling that he and it might be blended into one being. The world did not yet destroy this cobweb-work of fancy ; care and pain, which would have destroyed it, were absent. Selfish he was, having no check, and no object of equal sympathy ; selfish, and with no moral sense whatever; for how could he know that others desired to share his joy, when he saw nobody ? His poetic genius, born in no fiery throes, gradually woke to life in the quiet inter-change of summer and winter. But time brought growth of brain and thinking power, and these soon put a stop to his cobweb-spinning. He found himself living alone among his woodland sights. He began to see the true relationship between himself and them. Indiscriminate enjoyment of everything he saw began to be insufficient ; he desired to direct his energy of pleasure in some one or limited number of channels. How can I, thinks he, achieve this employment of my energy from the outer world of men, and having chosen my pleasure, enjoy it in imagination by proxy, and by sympathy, and so save myself the trouble of actual working to get it? **His** will had awoke; **it** drew him away from **simple love; his** judgment claimed **the enjoyment** *in imagination **only**,* and **by** force **of his will,** of attributes **of men.** His will **claimed** men's acknowledgment **of such his** power. **So for hi**m it was now an absolute **necessity** to live **before a** crowd. In the **host of men his** fancy **summons to** personate **the** crowd, **he discovers many attributes, some** which he **knew already,** more of which **he** had had no conception. He sees that in this crowd of men each has his own separate ideal, lives his **own** separate life. And in all these attributes, and in himself, no sign tells him which is good and which is bad. **His own pleasure then** shall decide **which of these he shall** use **and make** men acknowledge his power to use; and at length **he** concentrates such as his judgment decides are worthiest, being fain to hope that he himself will **by his own real** parentage and fortune prove to be equal **to the ideal** he has thus created. This ideal man is **greatest of** poets, greatest of kings, Apollo himself. An Apollo whom woods and trees, winds and skies, join together in worshipping; who triumphs over right and wrong, and draws the heart of all **the girls** of the earth out of their **old** loves into adoration of his transcendent Divinity. And when Apollo has satiated his soul with the fancy loves of

those who yield, he turns to the only real girl, who
scorning all other men, and having no old loves to
wrench away, has not yet paid to him her tribute
of worship. This girl is Palma. He waits, growing
grave and lean and pale with expectation and
desire, for a real crowd, a real stage, a real love.

BOOK II.

In this book we trace Sordello's development as
poet, and further development as man, by influence
of his commerce with living men in their joys only;
and the temporary demoralisation of the man-part,
and temporary extinction of the poet-part, by this
influence.

At last a day comes when Sordello's impatience
drives him wandering out, half fancying that he
would see and secure Palma at once. His ramble
brought him to Mantua walls, where were assem-
bled a *real* crowd, gay and laughing, round a pa-
vilion.

While he stood abashed and faltering at this
first sight of real men and women, who ought to
have yielded *him* homage, Eglamor, Boniface's
Chief Troubadour, came out, and sang to them.
Sordello, recognising in the story a fancy of his
own, sprang to Eglamor's side, and took up his

theme. When the maddening applause was over, his eye suddenly lighted on Palma,

> the very maid
> Of the north chamber, her red lips as rich,
> The same pure fleecy hair ; one weft of which,
> Golden and great, quite touched his cheek as o'er
> She leant, speaking some six words and no more.
> He answered something, anything ; and she
> Unbound a scarf and laid it heavily
> Upon him, her neck's warmth and all.

The magic of fancy, which had been arrested by his first glance at the real crowd, moved again under the touch of love, and he became unconscious of the outer world till he found himself back at Goito with a prize at his feet, learned that Eglamor was dead of grief, and that Palma chose *him* for her minstrel. He passed a week in delicious reverie, from which he awoke a new man. For hitherto his life had been passed in unexpressed perception, with no event which showed either directly or indirectly the effect of *actual* as distinguished from fancied *contact* with man and woman. Thus his thinking power had not been exercised at all, there being no occasion calling forth the *expression* of thoughts. He had only *perceived*, not *thought*. But here had been the first instance in which his mind had been called upon to influence other minds by the *expression* **verbally** of thought ;

and his mind being once set in that channel, its streams were henceforth divided; the pure stream of perception flowing still, side by side with the new and sometimes turbid stream of thought. He began to consider why he had beaten Eglamor. He proceeded to analyse the motives which impelled him to the first triumphant exercise of the poet-part of his Apolloship, and concluded that since his fancy made him actually love the subject of the song, as well as and above the act of singing, men who *applauded* his rhymes would surely *adore* his power of fancy. And as he arrived at this conclusion, Eglamor's corpse was borne towards him through the woods, to be buried far from the scene of his defeat. The trouveres were chanting at the head of the bier a song in praise of Eglamor. That song told Sordello how the art of verse was to Eglamor the worship of nature as a Divine power, the lifting of a veil, the performance of rites whereby some sound or sight of beauty, thus created, were fixed in rhyme, and made his own, to mix with his life and unloose at pleasure to ease pain and trouble. He was the priest of the temple, apart from all other men, freed from care for the world's coldness. Sordello, shaken by strong pity at the sound of the verses, took his own crown and laid it on Eglamor's breast.

Thus, then, had the two souls—Eglamor's the
first class mentioned in Book I., Sordello's fast developing into the second class—come into collision;
Eglamor's being the weaker, had been overcome.
But Eglamor's death taught Sordello's awakening
sympathies to embrace not only strength, but also
the tender beauty of weakness. For here was
Eglamor, needy, obscure, yet nursed in the hearts
of his own people. Can Sordello win such love,
supposing (horrid thought) that he may after all be
no real prince? He sternly determines before
doing anything else to learn who and what he is.
He finds that he is the reputed son of a common
soldier who had saved Adelaide and her child
when Taurello and Ecelin burned Vicenza.

His hope of kingship overthrown, he takes the
next step in his development. Thrown back on
himself and his qualities as simple man, irresponsible because unshackled by any grace or power
added by the world, why need he follow any
known example? He who does *not* act, is already
greater by virtue of *fancy* than those who *do* act,
who have a distinct purpose, which as a star guides
all their life; he can and will gain by his fancy all
the results which they by their action have striven
or will strive to get. 'My soul shall express the
essence of all beauty by its self-consciousness

thereof; and if the world can wonder at men who like Eglamor themselves wonder, and can idolise men who like Eglamor themselves bow to an idol, how shall it worship me, who neither wonder nor idolise, but express, by the self-consciousness of my soul, all that *is* wondered at or idolised. I will express by song all joys that are, without tasting one ; I will win from men the love which must be given to him who leads each man's soul to see the thing he most longs for.'

His plan thus made, he visits Mantua. There he is received with rapture, and begins to try and work out this new ideal by actual song.

He conquers his first repugnance to work, and achieves success sooner than he expected. Dazzled by its brilliancy, he for a moment shamefully longs for the very joys which it is his plan to abjure; but again bends to his work; and as influence over men by song is his first object, resolves to adopt the dramatic form.

Having remodelled his language, in his perception he creates a drama, and presents it in its *new* panoply of *new* language. But, alas! he finds that language, however modelled, is purely a work of thought ; that thought is a thing made of successive pieces, while perception is a thing whole and simultaneous—that by consequence, if on the one hand (in his desire to present the perception whole) he clothes it with thought, he hampers it **as much as** one would hamper a man **bred up to go** naked by clothing him with an armour **of** many **pieces.** Or, if on the other hand (in his desire to **show men** the perception at any cost), he presents **it in** successive pieces of thought, he is really only trying to show men what an entire thing is like, by first tearing it in pieces, and then presenting **the** parts successively for *them* to put together according to their knowledge. So, remembering **that** even if he could present the perception *entire*, this would be an impertinence, seeing that by **virtue of** his **will he could** *be* the perception—and seeing, moreover, that his audience was not likely **to** imagine anything higher than the highest idea he presented, which they praised already—he falls **back on** his old mode, and contents himself with **men's old praise,** thinking ' go further, fare worse.'

But here **he is** met by **a** new difficulty. What- ever **mode he** chooses, his audience decline **to** re- cognise in his portraiture his power by will to *be* the men he portrays; and seeing **in him** only an **ugly,** stunted, weakly minstrel, **insist on** giving him **praise for** his *rhymes*, and his **heroes** praise for their *deeds*, keeping each carefully distinct. This angers him. Why, he hotly asks, should he care

N

about the recognition of the Mantuans? His hope
of self-display by force of will (his poet-part) thus
thwarted, a division arose in Sordello. His man-
part, which insisted on immediate and adequate
reward for every piece of work, calmly tied up the
wings of the poet-part, and took its own way,
simply snatching any chance to secure *some* prize
which should by its brilliancy acquit the poet-part
of contempt. The poet-part being thus crippled,
its twin sister, the art of verse, by which Sordello
was to assert his Kingship, became virtually palsied
too. While the poet-part, ever struggling against
its bonds, perpetually called on him to stick to his
ideal, abjure actual joys, and compel the age to
know him, by force of his will producing self-re-
vealment, the man-part fiercely urged him to shake
off lethargy and timidity, and enjoy, while there
was time, mixing with men. But before he could
decide, the Mantuans, who cared nothing for his
doubts, threw him out of thought by their intru-
sions ; and he had no choice (having no time to
work out his thoughts) but to take a neutral
ground, and go in for a humdrum minstrel's life,
performing the every-day duties which fell to the
lot of Palma's troubadour. In this deep abase-
ment he met a new trouble; for he had to con-
verse : and could not at first do other than think

carefully out any topic proposed to him. Now the
Mantuans had all *their* opinions duly sorted, and
ready for immediate delivery; but Sordello, un-
trained as yet to speak half-truths sounding well,
could not give any immediate opinion otherwise
than by guess, which was as likely to be wrong as
not. So that on any topic started he was in this
dilemma: in the present turmoil of his double self,
he was compelled first to guess what effect his
speech would have on others; and then, to try and
represent in his speech what was passing in his
brain; and his conscience not being yet deadened,
disgust at the part he played outwardly made him
somewhat tardy in expressing any ideas at all.
Thus the total failure which ensued, unless he
could give birth to his idea at the moment, de-
moralised him, and the end was that he disgraced
his intelligence by giving out any common opinion
or saw as his own thought, without really troubling
himself to think at all. How, then, in this abase-
ment, could he care to take interest in men, for
love or hate of them? Here, too, he saved his
mind the trouble of thought by praising and blaming as others did.

To such a depth had he sunk as man; how then
did he fare as versemaker? As such he had to
keep his place against rivals, and succeeded to

some degree. His poet-part, however, still struggling with its bonds, insisted that it was not
enough for him merely to show the external view
of any subject; that he must give his strength full
play, root up the thought of the subject, and show
root and all.   This the Mantuans object to.   'You
are a bard,' say they, 'not a philosopher, and
where is the use of over-refining your thoughts?
this is of no use in poetry ; stick to common sense.
Not that we should restrict the poet, but the knowledge that he is one should be his sufficient reward.'   Such arguments, repeated *ad nauseam*,
maddened him like fleabites; he succumbed only
to get rid of the torture.   But even in his com-
plaisance, he was sometimes foiled, not divining exactly what drift of his thoughts the Mantuans
were pursuing; whence ensued blunders, which he
was forced to rectify by lies.

At last he sunk so low, that ·his will became
powerless, his fancy imbecile, and at the announce-
ment of an intended visit of Taurello's to Mantua,
he fled back to Goito.

BOOK III.

THE third Book treats of Sordello's further development as man, by the influence of renewed

commerce with inanimate nature; and by the influence of retrospection on the experiences of the two first developments; and his completion of the first circle, that of egoism, by attainment of his first desire for self-aggrandisement.

Goito, having got Sordello back again, speedily worked out of him all Mantuan thoughts and reminiscences. Men, whom he would have used as a machine to compass self-perception, by forcing his godlike half into clay which could only be convulsed, never transmuted, thereby, were all gone; and his will, finding that if it flowed at all, it must flow between bounds, retired back to its fountain-head, his soul.

Better, surely, he thinks, in his despair, to be unrevealed, than only part revealed; since men, who should have acted as the machine for displaying the power of his will, would not act as that machine, where was the good of trying to use his will at all?

> To need become all natures, yet retain
> The law of my own nature—to remain
> Myself, yet yearn . . . as if that chestnut, think,
> Should yearn for this first larch-bloom, crisp and pink,
> Or those pale fragrant tears where zephyrs stanch
> March wounds along the fretted pine-tree branch!
> Will, and the means to show will, great and small,
> Material, spiritual—abjure them all

Save any so distinct, they may be left
To amuse, not tempt become! and, thus bereft,
Just as I first was fashioned would I be!
Nor, moon, is it Apollo now, but me
Thou visitest to comfort and befriend!
Swim thou into my heart, and there an end,
Since I possess thee!—nay, thus shut mine eyes
And know, quite know, by this heart's fall and rise,
When thou dost bury thee in clouds, and when
Out-standest: wherefore practise upon men
To make that plainer to myself?'

So he passed a year alone, in torpid delight;
but conscious, at odd times, that he was torpid.
His trick of verse was gone;

One declining autumn day
Few birds about the heaven chill and grey,
No wind that cared trouble the tacit woods—
He sauntered home complacently, their moods
According, his and Nature's.   Every spark
Of Mantua life was trodden out; so dark
The embers, that the troubadour, who sung
Hundreds of songs, forgot, its trick his tongue,
Its craft his brain, how either brought to pass
Singing at all; that faculty might class
With any of Apollo's now.

The year
Began to find its early promise sere
As well.   Thus beauty vanishes; thus stone
Outlingers flesh: Nature's and his youth gone,
They left the world to you, and wished you joy.

One day, the marsh was buried by an earth-
quake, and Mincio became a lake in its place.

This incident roused him from his torpor, to think,
Is nature then subject to the same fate as I ?
                    No! youth once gone is gone:
·Deeds let escape are never to be done.
Leaf-fall and grass-spring for the year ; for us—
Oh forfeit I unalterably thus
My chance? nor two lives wait me, this to spend
Learning save that?   Nature has time to mend
Mistake, she knows occasion will recur—
Landslip or seabreach, how affects it her
With her magnificent resources?   I
Must perish once and perish utterly!
Not any strollings now at even-close
Down the field-path, Sordello! by thorn-rows
Alive with lamp-flies, swimming spots of fire
And dew, outlining the black cypress' spire
She waits you at, Elys, who heard you first
Woo her, the snow month through, but ere she durst
Answer 'twas April!   Linden-flower-time-long
Her eyes were on the ground ; 'tis July, strong
Now ; and because white dust-clouds overwhelm
The woodside, here or by the village elm
That holds the moon, she meets you, somewhat pale,
But letting you lift up her coarse flax veil
And whisper (the damp little hand in yours)
Of love, heart's love, your heart's love that endures
Till death.   Tush!   No mad mixing with the rout
Of haggard ribalds wandering about
The hot torchlit wine-scented island-house,
Where Friedrich holds his wickedest carouse,
Parading—to the gay Palermitans,
Soft Messinese, dusk Saracenic clans
Nuocera holds—those tall, grave, dazzling Norse,
High-cheeked, lank-haired, toothed whiter than the Morse,

Queen of the caves of jet Stalactites,
He sent his barks to fetch through icy seas,
The blind night seas without a saving star,
And here in snowy birdskin robes they are,
Sordello! here, mollitious alcoves gilt
Superb as Byzant domes that devils built!
Ah, Byzant, there again! no chance to go
Ever like august pleasant Dandolo,
Worshipping hearts about him for a wall,
Conducted, blind eyes, hundred years and all,
Through vanquished Byzant where friends note for him
What pillar, marble massive, sardius slim,
'Twere fittest he transport to Venice Square—
Flattered and promised life to touch them there
Soon, by his fervid sons of senators!
No more lives, deaths, loves, hatreds, peaces, wars—
Ah, fragments of a whole ordained to be!

In a strong agony, his spirit wrestles with that bitterest of all despair, more terrible than the remorse of a ruined gambler, which is reserved for those who, renouncing all pleasure for the sake of a higher prize, find, when they have lost it, that the joys they spurned have slipped from their reach for ever.

How much better, he raves, is the use of common men! for they blend what little they see with their limited being, and make it their own; they strive to blend with their body and soul what is alien to each, *so far only as they can*, but no further. And they therefore succeed. But what have *I*

required for *my* soul? Nothing less than the
blending of the world. Ah, bitter truth! My will,
which does comprehend the whole world, is chained
to a body so feeble that my ideal depended on my
body's renouncing the joys of the world, in order
that my soul and will might reveal them in full
power of imagination. Therefore I have failed.
Shall my ideal be worked out hereafter? Shame!
I myself might, perhaps, have worked it out, had I
watched still closer my human sympathies, and
traced them to their source. Why did I flee from
Mantua? Why did I complain that my will was
fettered, when all the time I myself allowed it to
remain inactive? All the time, with the full knowledge that I *could* have unravelled the human
mystery, I merely elaborated the surface humanity
casually brought before me, either in actual life or
by books, by the dim light given by my predecessors, when if I had struck one honest blow
myself, I should have brought the real flame forth
which would have given me clear light. My minstrel trade gave me men to see; my business was
to gain for myself all their *real* attributes, freed
from the clouds gathered on them by custom,
chance, or the blindness of myself or my books.
Thus was I hidden from the pageant which was
passing, which has passed, will not return, and

which I might have seen by exercise of a little
more will.   Let me get at least some impress of
the world through my will upon my consciousness,
even though I get it by tearing up and destroying
the whole of my past life, which is now like a
ruined and blasted flower-bud; better this than
leaving that past life lifeless, dormant, like (as it
were) a bulb lying dormant in the grasp of a
mummy.

At this point, Naddo the trouvere, breaks in
upon Sordello's meditation, and gives him a summons from Palma to come to Verona.   This summons Sordello obeys (in emptiness of heart and
desire to see his love).   On his arrival, Palma tells
him in minute detail, her past life, and winds up
with proposing a scheme whereby Sordello may be
made head of the Ghibellins, and espouse her.

Here, then, is the chance of actual kingship
which Sordello had dreamed of in his early Goito
days, and despaired of achieving.   He sees now
that no soul without external help from station
or riches is sufficient either in means or in *skill*
to work such means, first, for its own delight, and
displaying its will; and, second, for making men
recognise that will by display of powers.   He finds
also that his will, which, thus proved insufficient, he
had commanded to abdicate its throne, may still sit

on that throne, and suffer his soul to enjoy mankind, but in a way different from his first desire ;
that is, his soul may enjoy them, *not* by taking
their attributes, and in the exercise thereof com-
pelling them as subjects to render homage to the
display of power, but by taking them as independent beings and making them as a body act
out their faculties by the influence of his soul,
which he can bring to bear by the external help of
actual power. He therefore resolves to assume
his kingship and wield the mass of souls and
bodies entrusted to his care, even though in so
doing, he should have to live solitary, as the core
of the fruit is shut in by the rind. Thus is Sordello brought round to the fulfilment of the first
desire with which he started in life.

BOOK IV.

THE second circle of Sordello's life is occupied
with his development as an altruist; and in this
Book we shall trace his further growth as a man,
by the influence of renewed commerce with men in
their sorrows, and the elevation of his nature caused
by that influence.

In the interval between Sordello's departure
from Goito to Verona, Azzo and Richard had

stormed Ferrara, and Richard had been entrapped
by Taurello. Ferrara was torn in pieces by Guelf
and Ghibellin, and the mass of the people were in
great misery.

Sordello, on his arrival with Palma from Verona,
had visited Este's camp near Ferrara, had inspected
the crowd of great ones there, and his meditation
on the sight is pursued in Taurello's garden in
Ferrara. This crowd of great men and small
which he meant to task to its utmost by making it
act out as a body its various attributes by the influence of his soul — What were they, after all?
He saw the great men in luxury, he saw the small
men in misery; and he found that, as the shrubs
in Taurello's garden, which were passed over in
looking, drew his attention to the large trees, which
seemed made more prominent by the mediocrity
of the others, so the effect of his thoughts of the
multitude of undistinguished people who were only
looked at by his mind's eye in the mass, was to
make the very few *real* chiefs great only by the in-
significance and massing of that multitude which,
like the smaller shrubs, seemed arranged and un-
cared for. What pitiable herd of men was this,
which seemed to put a good face on its unimpor-
tant misery : certainly never thought of interfering
with Sordello's desired enjoyment of life; and by

its manner of taking any enjoyments it *had*, at once betrayed its good or bad estate? A great yearning of pity, working in his heart, brought up with new effect old Mantuan memories of all his early dreams of great men, all his after-dreams of making men work as a body to his soul; and, out of the old memory and the pity, was forged, before he knew it, a bond which fastened him to this poor mankind. He found that without any effort of his, and in a totally unforeseen way, mankind and he were really blended. For the misery he had seen called up in his imagination the misery of all poor men; a misery that bound its victims in a thrall more severe than the thrall of the weakness of his flesh. Here, then, was a body for his soul; not a body to do what his soul commanded, but a body chained by misery, and to be made free. So he turned from the joys of the few great, to observe the sorrows of the many little. This body of poor mankind should be made of equal privilege with those rich. He had erred greatly; he ought all this while to have thought of and tried to satisfy men's *wants*, not to claim their possessions, as his own. So he sighed deeper now, because of the fleetness of joy; for there was the people to care for besides himself. But seeing his past fault, he decided to try first the minor task of making these people happy, and to that end to confront Taurello; for there was surely an instant way to it, viz. by espousing whichever cause would bring the people most good.

Wandering through the city scarcely an hour after his interview with Taurello, he saw that through misery men and women were brought below love or self-respect, and that he himself was not safe from murder. He heard what seemed to show that men would slay their own kindred for their cause; and then the very (supposed) fratricide turned and asked him to 'drive bad thoughts away' by a song! Fain as he was to refuse, and hope that some real great one (Apollo) had the charge of this poor people, and thus get off the self-imposed responsibility to reclaim so lost a race, he retained still the power to build songs on the broad human nature; and so sang to them.

At midnight of that day, by a watchfire, Sordello learned of Palma that both Guelf and Ghibellin subsisted by the same injustice; and found to his dismay that whoso ranked with either must be a foe to man. Then I am absolved! says he. If *I* have done nothing, these have done worse than nothing. Nay, *I* had the notion of a service; what indeed else brought me here? Stay! what if there be a cause distinct from these, left for *me* to discover? (Here a watcher came to them, and told Sordello, as the subject for a ballad, the story of Crescentius Nomentanus; who in the absence of Pope John and King Otho, tried to restore Consular Rome. But the Pope and King returning in the nick, crucified him.) Rome, then, thought Sordello, shall be *my* groundwork; the two factions of Lombardy try after their manner to make a Guelf or Ghibellin Rome. I will make a new Rome, keeping the old in mind. And in the morning twilight he went forth to work out his plan among the people.

BOOK V.

HERE we find the revival of his poet-part by the renewed commerce with men in their sorrows; and his further development as man by the same influence, as evidenced by a fresh step in altruism, viz. the taking upon himself the stern practical task of an endeavour to make poor men happy.

In the evening of that day, having fully learned the hopelessness of trying to make this miserable rabble fit for his imperial city, and mourning over the fading of this last beautiful dream, a low voice arrested his ear. It said, 'Sordello, wake and listen! A man sees two sights: the first, the whole

work; the second, **the first step to** that whole work.
Why take **the end** instead of the beginning ? **You
were God in** conceiving **the whole** work; be man
now and take the first step. Remember that
collective outstrips individual man ; **and** apply
this principle to this dream of yours. Who first
sought **to work the** people's **good** by welding them
as a body to one soul ? Charlemagne, the incarnation of joy, thence unfeeling and therefore **strong,**
did it **by simple** strength, and men **were happy** so
far as **unity and irresistible** force could make them.
Go forward along the road of time, and you find
the peoples, already whole in strength, gradually
getting experience of **sorrow by the contests** caused
by that strength. **Out of the** accumulating mass
of that sorrow a soul arises which shall heal the
wounds of the body of strength, by its new attri-
bute **of knowledge. Hildebrand,** the incarnation
of sorrow and *knowledge*, **thence feeling, therefore**
stronger **than** Charlemagne, by his knowledge, **as**
the soul of **the peoples, wielded their** strength, **and**
made it work **to help** knowledge, **and so** made
men happier than Charlemagne could do by simple
strength. Hildebrand's work having conquered
and blended with Charlemagne's, both works proceed **by** instruments **of** whom indeed a few only
can be discerned now, but who still have furthered

the work of the people's happiness, each doing his own life's portion and no more. The next step, of overthrowing strength entirely and working *know-ledge* by knowledge to make the people happiest of all, cannot be taken yet; for we cannot yet do without strength; when we can, perhaps Sordello's dreams may be realised. Thus, then, are you shown how useless is the mad striving to overleap your life's work in order to achieve a result only to be got after ages of successive labour. If you *will*, spurn the notion of being only one of a series of workmen; fall back, forego all strife, and doze your life away in imagination. Only remember that you have given yourself to men to work for them. You have welded yourself and mankind into one being, they the body, you the soul. How then can yourself, the soul half, please yourself and men, your body half, by fancy only? Look at all the misery around you, and think; it is possible you are chosen by fate as her instrument to take the chances she has wafted to you for helping the work one step. Will you yet spurn these chances and advance upon the end? Go, persuade Taurello. If you fail, then—

But this was enough. He sprang up, determined on the side of mankind, and taking the Guelf cause as the National, and therefore the most just

one, proceeded to the chamber where Taurello sat
with Palma, in order to plead that cause before him.
When he first began his oration, he succeeded little,
not expressing in his speech the feeling which was
in his heart. Finding no visible effect from his
speech on Palma and Taurello, he became despe-
rate, fearing that he had lost all power to work or
express the need of it, thinking there was no alternative but to mope his life out in poet dreams.
But this his awakened conscience could not brook;
he began again. Taurello heard him patiently,
repeated his arguments for *Guelf*-domination to
Palma the Ghibellin, and asked her how they would
suit her, with a sneer at a poet taking up soldier's
or statesman's business. This contempt for a moment paralysed Sordello, but only for a moment;
the next instant he was stung by it into action
and resistance; out of his perceptions he answered
Taurello. For he felt that the people whose cause
he espoused were his judges, and would not let him
sink into carelessness; that if he succeeded now,
they would indeed make him king. What, thinks
he, have I forgotten my kingship, which I have by
virtue of my poetship?

> Thus I lay
> On thine my spirit and compel obey
> His lord—my liegeman—impotent to build
> Another Rome, but hardly so unskilled

In what such builder should have been, as brook
One shame beyond the **charge that I** forsook
His function! Free **me** from that shame, **I bend**
A brow **before,** suppose new years to spend,
Allow **each** chance, nor fruitlessly, **recur—**
Measure thee with the Minstrel, then, demur
At any crown he claims! That **I must** cede
Shamed now, my right to my especial **meed—**
Confess thee fitter help the world than **I,**
Ordained its champion from eternity,
Is much : but to behold **thee scorn the post**
I quit in thy behalf—to hear thee **boast**
What makes my own despair! **And while** he rung
The changes on this theme, the roof up sprung—
The sad walls of the presence-chamber died
Into the distance, or embowering vied
With far-away Goito's **vine** frontier ;
And crowds **of faces** (only keeping **clear**
The rose-light **in the midst,** his **vantage** ground
To fight their battle from), deep **clustered round**
Sordello, with good wishes no **mere breath,**
Kind prayers for him no vapour, since, **come death,**
Come life, he was fresh-sinewed every joint,
Each bone new-marrowed as whom gods anoint,
Though mortal **to** their rescue : now let sprawl
The snaky volumes hither!

'I have always been royal; if I fail now it is
because by trifling at first and **never** putting forth
the worth which being original **makes** me king, I
have been unworthy to hold **my** throne. My
power **to** profess all forms of **life at pleasure was, I**
thought, in its novelty, my proof **of kingship.** But

too late, I see this was not so, for I was but the copier of nature. Truly this power, as means to an end, does constitute that original worth which gives me kingship. What, then, is the end? It is that I might use this power to embody myself in men, that I might further use it to impress men with my soul, and that at last they may embody themselves in me. To achieve this object, would give me kingship. Thus should I live and move and have my being in mankind; thus should I secure for myself a crown which (when the world had taken my full essence) I would transmit to a successor more potent. Of such a race of kings I am one! Does pride of this elate me too much? No! for as my kingship consists in embodying myself in men and men in myself, by this process men are made equal to me; I am their brother, since by my words they have been brought to knowledge, and they and I have a better thing to satisfy us than mere deeds. For, as in the beginning, there was chaos, and to still the noise thereof Saturn emerged, so from the chaos of deeds has song emerged and was embodied in a poet, who like Saturn stilled the tumult and took throne supreme. And why is the poet supreme? Because his power of song is the fullest effluence of the finest mind; because his mind, different in

degree only from the other minds, has (instead of
keeping on level ground and taking one single
object to be gained, or to impress itself on as these
do) left behind all single objects, in order to attain
them collectively in the end. Do you ask how
has this attainment been achieved? I answer, by
thought; by the power of taking all acts by fancy
and representing them in words, and thus by the
influence of words, making men produce acts.
Thought is then to acts what the soul is to the
body. The poet disengages thought (the soul)
from acts (the body) and by exercise of his will,
not by acts of his own, makes men work, as his
body. How, then, shall I do the work of thought
by song? First, I will take simply evil and good,
and by strong contrasts of light and shade, show
you the chief of men in good and bad; I the
while, not standing above men but blending with
them and sympathising with them in their estimate of such my work. Then I will take such
men in good and bad and affect them by the circumstances of the world, showing how thus their
nature works. Then I will take as my audience,
not the whole world, but a few, and show *them* the
inmost life, the very beginnings of all human attributes in good and bad; till a time will come when
those few can do for all these stages what I did;

and we shall talk as brothers talk, discontinuing
old aids. For now we shall have a past to work
on; and we who are the judges, without appeal, can
by a touch of ours alter to great or little, and decide
the relative importance, of the structures of that
past. Then will the poet take a new step; he will
use what has been accomplished to create a new
structure; till the seal is razed from all the greatest
works, and poetry takes and shows the world all
their results as one result. But whoever achieves
this last grand work, labours like me for mankind;
he too, like me, must be content to express not a
tithe of what there is to say.

Thus having established my royalty, I cast away
fancies; I turn to the work of this moment; I bow
Taurello to the Guelf cause; content to die, now
first I estimate the boon of life, with the people for
my support!

Taurello, overcome by the flood of eloquence of
which the substance has been here feebly indicated,
takes a sudden resolve, and throws over Sordello's
neck Friedrich's badge, making him head of Romano; and proceeds to declare his plan, beginning
with Palma's and Sordello's espousals, but breaking off there. For without words the conviction
came on them that Sordello was Taurello's son;
which conviction Palma confirms by telling Ade-

laide's dying confession, **which there was now no need to conceal.**

Taurello having at length somewhat recovered from his first astonishment, proceeds to unfold his plan for subjugating the Guelfs, throwing **Fried-rich over,** taking Lombardy and keeping **it for** Sordello. Then, at that point, Palma took Taurello away, to give Sordello a chance of collecting himself and of thinking over the astounding fortune thus thrown in his path.

BOOK VI.

WE are now come to the last agony **of the great** fight, the last scene of this soul's tragedy. Sordello stands alone, face to face with a strong temptation. He has made his firm resolve to spend his life and **will** in getting joy for the people; he has roused his soul to superhuman eloquence in pleading that people's **cause** before Taurello; and **Taurello,** smitten with his fervour, has determined to draw this mighty power from the cause of freedom to the cause of tyranny, and by a sudden and commanding gesture, has thrust into his hands, will he, nill he, a great engine of power. The moment that act is performed, Palma discloses the secret of Sordello's birth, and adds tenfold to the force of the tempta-

tion by showing that he is what he first desired to
be, noble by parentage, born to rule. At this
critical moment, they leave him alone. And in the
solemn twilight, and in the bare presence chamber,
his soul stands up, fettered by his body, as a bull is
tied to the stake, to fight with the last grim enemy.

At his imperative summons, his past life came
before him, holding in its hand, for his light in the
combat, the lamp of truth. And now the fight
began. He hurled aside the lures presented to
him by the enemy, and looked steadfastly back.
So looking, he saw each effort was right, save
where it checked another; that his whole career
showed the existence in him of an all-embracing
sense which yet demanded some power above him,
as the moon is above the sea. But finding no
such power, and, consequently, no love, his all-embracing sense had wandered irresponsibly and he
had remained functionless. Thus he was inferior
to others who (with but half his strength) bowing
to a superior power, were able to fulfil their course.
Now Sordello had found no such power sufficient
to yearn to ; should he doubt, then, that he would
find such ? Or suppose there were no such power
for him, and he were reserved to be a law and a
love to himself ? Suppose *his* law, *his* love, should
be the necessity to remove all the incompleteness

which prevented him from securing the rest ? Suppose, indeed, all **such laws prescribed for** others were in **fact such a necessity, but in mercy to** weakness were embodied **in some shape or power for a lure?** Perhaps his vision was clearer, and he could endure to see the law, unclothed in any such **shape** or power. To test his strength **of** vision he **asked** himself, was he then less impelled to help **the** Guelfs **in virtue** of their *humanity* **than** he would have **been** impelled to help them **because** they were *Guelfs?* And if any how **he did help** the Guelfs, would he thereby be proudly **forsaking** the whole of **humanity** (that **is himself)? No!** serving a part **does not immolate the rest. He** must serve each part **in its due time.** A great scorn of his weakness in the purpose of helping the *present* **need of** the Guelfs **came** upon **him ;** this **present** need he had hitherto kept in view, **as** easier **than the** long task of wholly regenerating **all humanity. But** now, seeing that present **need,** he finds **how little his** service will do. Facing this truth, the Guelf woe, he is aghast to find **that the** small possible service he can do them will last a **lifetime.** But even while he sees the necessity for **fixing** this one **truth,** and that to fix it merits **crowning, he** cannot help mourning **that such effort is only** the striking **out** one stray spark of the entire

flame of truth which always lies buried somewhere,
and would, if loosed, right the world. ' But, at least,'
he cries, ' I will produce that spark ; throw over
Taurello's proposals, and thus attest my own belief.'

At this opportune moment, the enemy thrusts
before his eyes the badge, and bids him, before
he does this, think once more. Quoth the enemy,
' Is doing this *really* service ? Yes, in the end ;
but is 'it *now?* One sees the ultimate effect; but
the intervening causes are not so plain. If, indeed,
to-day's work were as clear in evidence of good as
the life's work ! To maintain the Guelfs in rule
(your life's work) is, past doubt, right ; but one's
day's work must be tempered to the natures one
has to deal with; and those natures must be moved
according to the end in view ; i. e. as they impede
or not the Guelf rule. If, indeed, each man proclaimed by outward mark his tendency, 'twere well
enough, but alas! the future of a cause duly determined has never been held to be superior in claims
to the undetermined wants of the present. Shall
you then smite or spare on a warrant so slight as
your future end gives you ? Break your present
sympathies, bear your present aversions, merely for
such a feeble end ? This were work indeed, but at
cost of other work ; shall you spoil a half-completed
orb to get a new quarter of an orb ? Rise one step

with the people, and sink one **yourself, or not one
step** only, **but** utterly? **Are old faith and** courage
wrong **because they were born from a wrong cause?
Surely we see on all** hands **evil beautified.** Shall
we then, to banish evil, destroy **beauty? Is evil a
less** natural result than good ? **For, if** you overlook
animal life and *its* evil (and whoso tries **to pry into
that finds nought** but a grinning taunt for solution)
and care for men only, you **can** but see **that good
and** evil claim **you** alike. **Does not the Guelfs'**
claim **rest upon evil?** If they **had no** sorrow, how
could **they claim your** help? What happiness could
you distinguish **in the miseries you saw this morning?** None **but a fool's,** who passed **a jest upon you
for a** Ghibellin ; and much hold he **took on you by**
his happiness! Nay, **on** men's own account evil
must stay; else can there be **no joy,** which consists
in removal of evil, and is itself **a** partial death, **being
the** freeing **of the** soul's essence from some **small
sphere, merely to** enter a larger sphere and **crave**
new enlargement. **Who** among men had **the world**
perfect, and **free** from obstruction? **Sordello** himself at Goito, who was disgusted **with** the perfection
and smoothness. There is **salvation in** every hin-
drance. Men *must* climb; they are not caught up to
the height, without wings, **to** see the view at **once;**
that view is laid **lower;** and the higher men climb

the more they see, heartened by each discovery; they seek the whole in parts; if they found it at once, where would be the enjoyment of retrospect, of past gains? Nothing would be gained but leave to *see*; there would be nought to *do*; for looking beneath soon sates the looker; looking above tempts only to die. Then, Sordello, live first, and die soon enough; feed on the shame that you are not vilely lodged with Lombards, but can force joy out of sorrow, and while you seem to barter your attributes for filth, get gold from that filth. For, though you get gold, it is only from what the world discarded; what would remain filth did you not touch it; and if you were to share the gold thus got with the world, you would simply be ruined, and the world not saved. Why then should sympathy make you give up joy, when the world's woe would not thereby be removed? For would *all* get joy? No. Then do not try to force all into joy, before they are ready for it; and thus thwart your own soul, which is ripe for joy. All will achieve joy at last; and let their time come as soon as possible—but think how you could achieve joy at once by this badge!'

The tempter had fought warily; Sordello was yielding. He felt that his time of action with reference to the world had in it a power of joy.

gigantic compared with the **pigmy** impotence **of** the **world to** profit **even at the** expense of that joy. **He turned his** back **on the** light of truth, **and** cried in **his** darkness, **'Shall I, because** my **time is short, make** nothing **of it? I will** rather use **grief,** taste vice (that **I may be eaten** through **with** life). Time indeed may reason out these as mischiefs hereafter, **but** I shall be gone. The **few who** stir are a match for the many who rest. **Let me be** employed then, and even though men suffer **by my** employment, **'tis but one pang for** each. **Who,** with Rome in **prospect to govern,** *can* sit **still?** Let me have **life first. What, shall** I wait for some transcendent **life to** follow this? No! **I trust my soul for** the after-life to fate. **For** if it was so easy for her to **make for me** so gorgeous a thing as this present **life, what** wonder if, **when that** is shrouded by death, she can throw **before my soul a** second and superber spectacle? What **future joys** can recompense **me for** giving up present **joys?** Does fate bid me drink at the rivulet by **my side,** or say nought **is** worth drinking save the fount **at** the mountain's **top? I** will serve the crowd, if thereby I do good; if not, why require **it of me? If** men must set **life** aside (and give it **to me)** why should I refuse the gift? I engage **never** to repent of having used **it.** Suppose the

world *is* a mere ante-room to a palace, why should
I become courtier before the due time? Why
should I forego the luscious pleasure of that ante-
room? Why, when I am admitted to the presence
and the new joys, should I have cause to grieve
that I have not tasted the old joys? Should I be
blest now if heaven came before earth? No! Let
me have stronger limbs; but I want no wings: Let
heaven be peopled with Titans, not men!—Yet stay
a moment; (he turns towards the light again) 'how
is it that the full cup of life, whose extreme dregs I
so long for, has been dashed aside so oft? Show
me what it was the martyrs renounced, what it was
which they found to master life, and I will do as
they did. As it is, I feel; am what I feel, know
what I feel; why must only one side of life (the
gloomy one) be right? What is abstract right for
me? It is (and he turns away from the light again)
that my youth is endowed with power to exist in
every mode of being, whether as king or slave.'

But here his past life gently stole again upon this
world-worn fighter, and soothed his eyes once more
with that gentle light. He cast himself out of the
enemy's arms into the deep yearnings of his soul's
essence; the chain of the flesh grew weaker, the
truth-light burned clearer, the enemy waxed fainter.
His soul said within itself: May it not be that good

and evil, great and small, are only modes of time, not of force, to bind eternity as they bind time, not of force, to bind mind as they bind matter? The fleshly chain **was** gradually weakening; the soul **began to** feel the earthly surroundings fading from beneath it, leaving it quite alone; the enemy had **sunk** into the gloom.

Sordello, out of time and the world, turned in **the** last moments to ask, 'What made the secret of my past despair? Despair which was keenest, which seemed most imminent; when my soul was maddened with struggles to expand and use its power, *not* **by craving** more **power?' And one** voice answered : 'This was the secret : **If the soul,** which is thrust as a prisoner into the body, tries that body beyond its straining point, sorrow comes. **Do** you ask, how avoid sorrow? You are thus answered. The sphere of this life, whether great **or** small, **was** nevertheless, being a thing with bounds, **a** prison to the absoluteness of the soul ; the only way **to** have avoided sorrow in the life which you have lost was to match the infinite soul's efforts to the **body's** finite powers, and whenever **the** soul's powers strove to transcend the bounds of the body, to lull the impatient Titan to sleep.'

Thus, then, was the dreamer's despair accounted for, and put away with the past. Thus did Sordello's soul, which transcended eternity, the whole series of spheres, learn in the bitterness of death, its incompleteness for time, the one sphere.

But does knowledge extend no further in the present life than this ? No, the battle is over; the. chain is broken; the winged soul has shot up beyond the clouds, and is free. The earthly Sordello is dead, with the badge beneath his foot. He knows now, but he is gone ; the hermit bee, which has fashioned his house this eventide by God's counsel, and will wake to-morrow to do God's counsel, knows here the secrets of this life sooner than Sordello, who will wake no more.

Such is the history of the life and death of Sordello; thus we have seen how in the second circle of his life (as in the first), he came back, before he died, to the aspiration with which he started, that of helping, even by self-sacrifice.

But it would not be right to dismiss the poem without entering on an enquiry into the nature of such a soul as Sordello's, its use for the Italians, and its use in the world.

This enquiry would, perhaps, be hardly necessary, if idealists only were likely to study the poem ; for they would all be ranged on the side of Sordello, and would almost by intuition, at any

rate by sympathy, be only too ready to exalt his
worth. But to realists, one feels that some apology
is necessary for the earnestness with which we lay
stress on the royalty of this poet soul, whom they
may call a poor dreamer, but whose life and whose
dreams were, perhaps, not so utterly useless after
all.

A realist would probably say something of this
sort : You have shown me a man who, till he was
near twenty, never saw a responsible human being,
whose boyhood was in luxurious ease, free from all
moral restraint, and doing, to all appearance, no
more brainwork than a butterfly. This man, when
he first came into contact with men, saw no better
end than to magnify himself in their eyes ; and,
on being baffled in this object, turned away like a
craven child, and cried himself to sleep in his
mother Nature's lap. He was only dragged out of
this shameful retreat by the weakest of all passions
for a gold-haired girl; and her intoxicating words,
and nothing else, roused him to do something,
which yet was to be only a repetition of his former
attempt to aggrandise himself. His first sight of
misery and suffering was sufficient to turn his weak
stomach sick, to unnerve his boastful purpose, and
change him to a dreamer more pernicious in his
influence than before, since now his dreams went

to make other men mad besides himself. He did, indeed, make one strong effort in the direction of helping the world ; but his self-introspection had so enervated the power of his brain for practical working, that he was entirely unable to make his hearers comprehend his meaning, and the only effect of his oratory was to raise a wonder and bewilderment in Taurello, which resulted in that statesman's seeing that here was an instrument fit for his purposes, an engine powerful indeed when set in motion, but utterly irresponsible, and which could be made work in any direction if only managed aright. Acting on this estimate of Sordello's character, Taurello, scorning the remonstrances of the helpless enthusiast, and ignoring the possibility of his having any groundwork for his ideas for the people, actually invested him, with no resistance on his part, 'with the headship of the very party which he was seeking to overthrow ; such investing having for its object the gaining of Sordello as a powerful engine to work *on the side* of that party, break faith with its supporter the Kaiser, and domineer in conquered Lombardy. Sordello, it is true, went through a final struggle with this temptation, but all his nature roused itself to force him to yield to it, and only death saved him from the unutterable disgrace of passing his days as Taurello's tool and Palma's plaything. Such is the man, to dissect whose nature we are called upon to wade through an obscure and clayey slough of dreary verses, the very grammatical construction of which it tasks our utmost energies to master!

Now the realist looks to see every day of a man's life turned to some account; to see every act of his produce some result of good, actual tangible good, either for himself or the world; he will have no dreaming; his cry is perpetually Do, Do, Do! And yet one may perchance show how every day of Sordello's life *was* turned to account; how every act of his *did* produce some good, actual tangible good, either for himself or the world; how although it must be admitted he did dream, his dreams were productive of quite as much result as, nay, of far more result than, if he had been occupied his whole life in doing, doing, doing. It is true that till he was near twenty, Sordello never saw a responsible human being; that his boyhood was passed in luxurious ease, free from all moral restraint, and doing to all appearance no more brainwork than a butterfly; but one must remark at the outset that if this is stated as an objection, the statement assumes one of two things; either it assumes a man's right to protest against the existence of such a nature at all, or else it leads to the inevitable conclusion that Sordello's boy-

hood was passed uselessly. As to any right to protest, we must take the world and the men in it as
we find them; it is worse than folly to object to
the existence of any particular form of nature,
seeing it is but a part, as we ourselves are, of a
great whole; and it is as absurd for one part of a
scheme to object to the existence of another part
of that scheme as it would be for the wheels of an
engine to object to being moved by the piston of
the engine; so that any such protest can only lead
to the conclusion that the uprooting of the offensive
nature is desired, which is probably a step too far.
As to the other alternative, that Sordello's youth
was passed fruitlessly, we will deal with that more
at length, and will seek some reasons to show that
the objection is groundless.

Now Sordello was plainly a poet in two senses;
first, an Italian poet for the Italians; second, a poet
for the world; and he was besides, in the course of
his life, both egoist and altruist. Let us consider
him first as an Italian poet for the Italians.

We know from the poem somewhat of the life
of the Italians; how under their hot sun their
brain ripened, so to say, into a double fruit; the
one half being composed of hatred, vindictive-
ness, intrigue, ambition of the aggrandising sort,
a cool and devilish power in diplomacy; the other

half being warmed with a passion for art, love, and
all forms of material beauty, which made it a necessity of their very being to have their unexpressed ideas embodied for them in song or pictures. We have also seen from the poem how the
artistic half of the Italian always influenced his
truculent half for a good end, if only circumstances
gave it a chance of infusing its gracious sweetness
into the other's gall; how without the mysterious
influences of poetry, painting, and music, to act as
gracious excitements in their daily life, that hot
blood of theirs would boil up so fiercely in the
quarrels and intrigues to which they were already
too prone, that nothing short of extermination
seemed capable of stopping the demon's course;
how, to use a more homely simile, poetry, music,
painting, were to them what icebags are to the
throbbing head of a fever patient. They needed
soothing by the music of verse, softening by its
inexpressible tenderness, training to thought and
gentleness by its imagery. All the poets who
should produce these happy effects were of the
same Italian blood, and none was more conspi-
cuous during his short life for the power he displayed, in this direction, over his countrymen, than
Sordello. Imagine thrusting Sordello, the Italian
poet, *in his boyhood*, into that turmoil of human

life! Remember how his fancy power, absolutely
destitute of knowledge of good and evil, seized only
too eagerly on any object even of inanimate nature
to tire itself upon. How would it have run riot
had fate thrown it thus early into the maddening
human life, so infinitely more bewitching to a
young and ignorant mind than any flower or tree,
however lovely! The river of human passions,
violent, turbid, foul as southern blood could make
it, would inevitably have drawn to it that broad
limpid stream, and, mixing with and discolouring
its pure water, would have overflowed on all sides
to spread ruin on every hand. Sordello, if bred
among men from a child, would have prevailed
over the Italians by his magic fancy, like some tremendous fiend-king, rousing all their worst passions,
crushing all their noblest sympathies. But put
such a soul under the gentle nursing of nature, and
his soul would quietly wake into being amid com-
panions who knew no intrigue, flowers who never
went mad for love, birds who knew no voice but
that of singing, trees and hills, skies and clouds,
who looked on as calm judges, not to try sin and
strife, but to tell poor humanity that silent and
passionless as they stood, they hid a mystery which
all the plotting of the world could not unravel.
Amid such teachers, and such teachers alone, could

Sordello, a young poet who was to work among a
people like the Italians, learn that reverence which
is the beginning of knowledge; here only could he
be led to yearn undefiledly, unchecked, unblinded,
after truths too deep for the greatest masters; here
only could he learn that calm strength of hand
which could soothe the feverish Italian into rest
from intrigue, and exalt him from rapine and lust
into graciousness and love; and here only could
he thus have developed in him that force and
straining power which should drive him to seek
things too high to attain, here alone could the
spirit of prayer develop itself, which, above all
powers, can lead any man to influence over his
fellows. Thus, then, was it well for Sordello, as an
Italian poet, that he remained untouched by the
world until his soul had attained vigour enough to
meet its rebuffs, until his fancy's wings were strong
enough to bear him in transcendent flights above
the worshipping eyes of his countrymen.

Looking at Sordello as egoist and poet, and
afterwards altruist, in his influence on the world at
large, and starting with the acknowledged fact that
his poetic faculty was of original growth and of
a supreme order, it appears to be the fact that the
nature of a great and *original* poet involves in its
earlier stages of development a strange paradox.

It is during its youth, on the one hand too intrinsically powerful to depend for sustenance upon any other mind ; and on the other it is in its very essence sympathetic to the utmost, and in commerce with men is far more apt to draw into itself and embody in itself all the natures with which it comes into contact, than to lean on them, or sink its individuality in theirs. Now the consequence of this is obvious ; such a soul generally starts with a gigantic power of enjoyment, a power which is far too strong for tender motherly dogmas to restrain, and which, therefore, impels it in the direction of securing present happiness, first actually and directly for itself, and then indirectly by bestowing favours and smiles on others ; the object always being to supply food for that rapacious monster, its own individuality. Such a tendency, coupled as it always is with vast powers of attracting, and winning to itself the hearts of others, may, nay must be of pernicious influence (in view of the absence of a morality above hinted at) both to the poet's self and the world. Such a nature being then strong enough to support itself, is much more strengthened, in its earlier development, if thrown upon itself for resources, and untempted save by distractions independent of notions of right and wrong, and untainted by the suggestions (which

a day's intercourse with men would produce)
teaching the knowledge of good and evil, than
it would be if thrown upon men for resources,
taught by them what is evil and what is good
in this world, and not only continually diverted
from its own originality by the sight of and con-
trast with the qualities of other men, but also
perpetually shaken and undermined by the ever-
recurring torment of questions whether this or that
thing is *right*, or worse still, whether the universal
voice of men is just in calling this thing good and
that thing evil. For such a soul, which in its
earlier stages is so easily affected by the working
of the imagination ; for such a soul, which takes
and absorbs all things with which it comes in collision, as an opal drinks in colours, what fate can
there be in store, if all humanity is drawn into its
essence, save a terrible chaos of discords and har-
monies which in their never-ceasing battle must
inevitably tear to pieces the goodly temple they
have so profaned ? What, in short, can be the
effect of too early contact with men, if not either
to destroy the soul utterly in its originality, to
warp its powers in any direction in which associations may lead it, or unduly to cramp those
powers by the effect of the necessary crowding
which must ensue where a number of minds jostle

on all hands one which is not so fixed and set,
and therefore not so strong, as they ?   Just as one
having a rare tree or shrub, would not in its sap-
linghood set it, on the one hand in a close planta-
tion of other *common* shrubs or young trees of its
own age, nor on the other in a forest of full-grown
giant trees; but would plant it carefully apart,
surrounded with all gentle influences to foster its
growth, in a green garden spot of spices and trick-
ling fountains, in a bountiful and prolific soil, where
skies were gracious, showers soft, and breezes
amorous—where no storm could ravage, no thunder
terrify, and no lightning scathe it ; so should the
young and royal poet be fostered.   His soul is a
thing too precious to run any risk of the pollution
or deformation which too early contact with the
world of men and women, old and young, virtuous
and godless, is sure to produce ; too precious to
allow the chance of its total ruin or destruction by
the thunder and lightning, the wind and storm, of
passion, war, or calamity.   Let it be gently dandled
to rest night after night by the strong soft hands
of the great inarticulate mother whom we call
Nature; let it find mystic speech in winds, in the
song of birds, in the brooding of the sky—let it
learn first kindliness—next positive delight—next
reverence—next perception.   And when, thus nur-

tured, it has attained full **growth, then, just as you**
would delight to set your **rare tree, now** full-grown,
among **a crowd of** other **full-**grown trees, **that so**
its beauty might be more effulgent **by reason of**
the commonness and dulness of the **rest, so** with the
full-grown soul ; you shall, if **you will,** lead it **forth**
to **do battle** with the forces of the world of **men, to**
use the strength thus nursed in solitude, to be self-
reliant in its strength, and **to** extract from all sights
and sounds about it, fresh **food** for self-development. And, at last, the development **of self will**
be complete, and the full-armed full-muscled **god**
will be ready **to** do battle not **for** himself **but for**
others, and **do** his endeavour, **successful or not, to**
help them to the happiness which **he** can see
clearly. And whether his career be successful or
unsuccessful, **his** purpose will be honest, **his** forces
rightly applied ; if he triumphs, the world will gain
a great champion and much prosperity ; if he fails,
the story of his hard-fought battles will go down
through the centuries ; and whether they who read
that story be **few** or many, a life spent to its last
blood-drop in **such** honourable striving will have
set its seal side **by** side with the **impress of** other
such strifes **on** the tablets whereon **are** sealed all
the battles and discords, all the peaces and har-
monies, which **go** to make up the sphere of the

great order, and in the mystic records lying hid in the secret places of that unknown God who is the master spirit of universal humanity, those few who are His chosen will read the story, so sad, so joyous, of a life which has been staked and lost.

Thus was it well for Sordello, as poet and altruist, that his nature did not too early contract the stain, the warpings, the crookedness of the world: thus was it well for the world that though his life was an unsuccessful one, it was pure in purpose, true to the end. And had it not been such, should we now enjoy the privilege of examining the precious treasure which the great English Master has dug out for us?

But is it true that Sordello, when first he came into contact with men, saw no better end than to magnify himself in their eyes, and that on being baffled in this object, he turned away like a craven child, and cried himself to sleep in his mother Nature's lap?

Now if it was well for Sordello in childhood both as Italian poet, as world poet, and as man, to be nurtured apart from the whirl of human life; if the Italian nature needed the soothing and elevating power of poetry; Sordello, nurtured as he was (his power of fancy being an acknowledged fact), was a poet well able to govern the intellectual and sensuous qualities of the Italian nature. But as, in this part of the subject, we have only as yet considered Sordello's early youth, it will be well to examine his further development, not only as a great Italian poet for his influence on Italians as such, but also as a great poet and as a *man* for the benefit of the world. And it will probably appear that for all these further developments it was good for Sordello that the first half of his soul's earthly life was passed as an egoist. In short, while admitting that Sordello saw no better end, in this beginning of his life, than to magnify himself in men's eyes (which is another way of saying, what has been said already, that he was at first a great egoist) it now becomes necessary to show that it was this quality of his, this monstrous egoism, which really made him eventually so supreme. Let us then look into the reason of this egoism. The man knew so soon as he came into the society of human beings, as all such men must know, that his imagination and fancy were regal in comparison with those of other men ; the natural consequence was that until he was measured against other men in actual contact, he must assume supremacy over them, and desire to make them acknowledge him. When he saw then the royalty of his imagination, and desired to assert it in actual supremacy, what would he first seek for as most likely to bring about the accomplishment of his

desire? Surely he would seek for an opportunity
to display his power in order to the assertion of
such actual supremacy. And on his obtaining such
an opportunity, whether he succeeded or failed in
it, what would be the next result to him? His
purposes being as yet, by reason of his pure nature,
quite guileless, he would naturally use his power
(whether he had succeeded or failed in his first
attempt) in the direction of making himself stronger
still. For if he had succeeded, his lively imagination, unslaked, would desire more power; if he had
failed, his courage, yet undimmed by perpetual
reverse, would even more hotly urge him to new
efforts in the direction of self-development—self-
development which had for its object at first
merely the rightful assertion of superiority.

Thus, then, it seems extremely probable that the
nature of a supreme mind such as Sordello's was,
nurtured as Sordello's is shown to have been, is
first to claim and assert supremacy, and then to
strive after self-development to that end. Having
seen how the first step, the assertion of supremacy, is either achieved or at least attempted,
let us see how the second step, the strife after
self-development to that end, is carried out. It
appears that the nature of a supreme imaginative mind of a great poet is such that it is

governed in its exercise of imagination, *mainly* by the things itself sees, only in a minor degree by the things heard or read ; and again, yet another quality in the nature of such a supreme imaginative mind is a yearning out of itself for sympathy and love, a magnetic influence which draws other natures into it, which yearning and tendency, egoistic as they are, have in them something divinely altruistic, since they show the necessity for a blending with other natures and making them happy. With these qualities then to work on, how is the strife after self-development carried on by such a soul as Sordello's, when first transported into the full glow and fragrance of all human beauty; when transported, as Sordello was, into the midst of luxury, wealth, and happiness? Such a soul surely must turn the whole force of its powers towards self-development in the delineation and enjoyment of these glorious things, beauty of sight, and sound, and smell, and touch, all blazing and breathing upon its fine perceptions. How should it remember sorrow and suffering, the portals to altruism, terrible phantoms shrouded from sight, and therefore left out of the question as things unknown or only heard of, and therefore half believed ?

Such a soul as Sordello's, lapped in human pleasure, yet still kept pure not only by its own

innate nobility but **by** that very desire after supremacy which **we** have seen **to** predominate, **is**
impelled, **the imagination being** still supreme, **to**
make gigantic strides **towards** the highest in whatever **of the** things **seen it attempts to master.**
These things seen are, as shown, the things **of joy**
only, because of that supremacy of the imagination ;
and all the soul's **att'empts in the** direction of joy
must, **from the nature of its** present egoism, be
attempts **in the direction of its** own pleasure and
aggrandisement. **But are such attempts enervat-**
ing in their effect, as being egoistic, as having
luxury for their end ? No ; the purpose is still
pure ; self-development is still the goal, its efforts
urge the **soul not to rest and ease, but to** new **toil,**
which toil, **from its very nature,** must result in the
absolute **strengthening of fibre.** The soul proceeds,
daily **gaining power, daily** nourished **by joy ; and**
still redoubling **its efforts for itself,** it increases
fourfold its **power.**

Since then it is the **necessity of the soul to strive ;**
since rest even for **its own ease** is out of the question,
the power must **go on increasing.** And how is
that power eventually **to be** exercised ? Not on
itself, for that would be self-destruction, which
would be as much out of the question as rest. No :
the power must eventually be exercised, for an

engine to influence men. But until this stage is reached, the egoist must go on developing step by step, until he meets, as he must do, some tremendous rebuff. And now the first real test of his strength begins. His muscles are now mighty, and he opposes force with force. But he finds that the joyful world is, through excess of that joy which he is striving to learn, hard and unfeeling, and is stronger in its buffets than he is who is only working his way up to joy, and who is not unfeeling but sympathetic, though as yet unknowing how to use his sympathy. He gradually gets exhausted, but he does not get really weaker, because all through the battle that sympathy which perhaps weakened the force of his strokes at the time, was a power in him reserving his strength for other and greater combats, a power which would permeate his being like the breath of God. But now, what wonder if, utterly blown and strengthless, he at length sinks beaten in a hopeless combat? Has he shown want of courage? Are his forces ebbed away? No! He is merely faint from loss of blood; when he goes away to recruit himself, the sympathetic spirit will, unknown to him, begin to nourish his being, and to nerve his courage for new attempts; give him time, and he will be stronger than ever he was before. All that training which he has undergone, and which is directed only on himself, has developed him to such a degree that, helped by his powers of sympathy, his force must turn into some other channel, if as is Sordello's case, the purity of purpose is unstainable, and since, as is also Sordello's case, rest or self-destruction is also impossible. Thus then is this egoism a blessed engine for future use, a fitting of the man for strifes greater than this was, when it shall be not himself he fights for, but a cause of which as yet he knows not the existence—the cause of all mankind. Thus the true supreme imaginative soul must by necessity be an egoist, until he is strong enough and responsible enough to take his post as an altruist; and if Sordello was baffled at first, he came back and fought like a man till he saw that victory was hopeless at present.

As to the objection' that Sordello was only dragged out of his shameful retreat by the weakest of passions for a gold-haired girl; and that her intoxicating words, and nothing else, roused him to do something which yet was to be only a repetition of his former attempt to aggrandise himself; let us take up the thread where it has just been dropped.

Sordello, who was no craven when he sunk beneath the buffets of the world, but was only a

tired fighter acknowledging **nobly a real** defeat
and retreating to recruit his shattered strength ;
when he **awoke** refreshed **in** Nature's lap, justified
our estimate **of** the necessity **of his nature to be**
always striving. For as a true fighter, having re-
covered from the blows **of his** battle, begins again
to train himself, so did Sordello, awaking, take up
the struggle with his own mind, and win the victory
over his temptation to yield and be lazy ; **so did**
he train his muscles **anew for** another fight. **And**
since **it was the** necessity of his supremely imaginative mind **to yearn** out of itself **for** sympathy
and love, Sordello, egoist still, **when he went out**
at Palma's bidding **to** cope again **with the world,**
to try another fall, was too true **to** check his nature
in any worthy attribute ; **and** while keeping his
thoughts on the coming battle, did not **think it**
shame **to** give the rein to the first efforts **of his ·**
soul **towards** sympathy and altruism, even though
displayed **in the** love for a woman.

We have seen how egoism **is** good, and **how it**
must be existent **up to** a certain point when **a** man
sees only joy, **and no** sorrow, **in** other men ; and
indeed the time **for** real altruism was **not** come
yet. The great egoist must **go on** increasing **in**
strength and skill, **all** his efforts **now** being guided
and nourished **by his power of** sympathy, and

tending towards the development of his sympathy
with mankind, at present represented only by Palma.
The power of sympathy led him towards Palma.
The scheme she proposed to him showed him a
chance of self-development (for the egoist was not
yet complete), but it also showed his new awakening altruist power a chance of influencing men,
in an egoistic way certainly, but still in a way far
more compounded of sympathy with men than his
former efforts had been. It is clear, then, that
hitherto all his efforts were really in a right direction, that at least it is not unreasonable to say that
Palma's scheme only showed him a way which he
could not know before, to achieve certain victory
over the world in his next battle with it. We
may, therefore, conclude that he was absolutely
and entirely right in listening to her words, and
preparing to embrace her scheme, since though it
did seem in one view to tend towards his own
aggrandisement, he did not forget that men were
to gain benefits by the achievement of that very
end.

Sordello's first sight of misery and suffering was
indeed sufficient to turn his weak stomach sick,
to unnerve his boastful purpose, and change him
into a dreamer; but whether this dream were
more pernicious than before, since it went to

make other men mad besides himself, is open to doubt. Let us again take up the train of thought traced down to this point. Sordello, as an egoist, has attained the highest possible position. The nature of his soul, as already seen, could never have been satisfied in any circumstances with supremacy in the direction it had followed hitherto, because such supremacy would imply rest, which was alien from his nature. We have also seen the existence, as a fundamental attribute of Sordello's character, of the yearning of sympathy and love. Even supposing, then, that as an egoist he had met perfect success, such success would have palled upon his soul, and it would have cast aside its crown, descended from its throne, and turned for new food to use men for themselves, instead of for itself, in pure honesty of purpose; while the very nature of that new employment would develope to its highest his sympathy and altruism. Had he met with ill success, his honest undaunted struggles with repeated failures and rebuffs had now so strengthened the fibres of his soul, that it would have been able to maintain the fight, and see where its force was ill applied; and its power being now redoubled by the alliance of the full-grown angel of sympathy, it would now take stand as so far above the crowd, and yet so intuitively

alive to their nature, that hostility, so often the sign
of weakness, would be unnecessary; he would be
strong enough to turn the fight into an embrace by
a single gesture; and in due season (not when it
was too late) he would have changed his tactics,
and converted the enemy into a worshipping friend
by offers of love and even of help. As it was,
however, the full-grown egoist had no such slow
process to go through in order to reach altruism;
for without requiring him to engage in any further
struggle, fate graciously wafted him full materials
on which to work his now renewed and redoubled
strength; in his self-part, heart and brain were
fully developed; and behold, that ever-youthful
Titan, dewy-eyed, fronted like the morning, called
altruism or sympathy with mankind, was awakening rosily in his chamber, and the twofold Sordello
was ripe to cast his whole gigantic force into the
cause of curing sorrow and weakness. Because his
soul wept at the first sight of calamity, was he
therefore weakened by such weeping? Because
he was a poet, and as such, a dreamer, must his
dreams be therefore pernicious? Have we not
acknowledged his power as a poet? Have we not
seen how useful and how necessary he was to the
Italians as such? how, then, otherwise than as
Poet, could his power be exercised? Were his

dreams pernicious because they turned in the direction of freedom for **slaves?** If it were pernicious
to dream how to rouse **the Guelfs, the** real lords **of**
the soil, into a strife for freedom from the **Saxons,**
if it were pernicious to dream how to drive **famine**
and plunder away, and bring home plenteousness
and peace—the absurdity answers itself.

But if it is still objected that, although Sordello
did indeed make one strong effort in the direction
of helping the world, his self-introspection had **so**
enervated **the** power of his brain for practical
working, that he was utterly unable **to** make **his**
hearers comprehend his meaning, and that the **only**
effect of his oratory was to **raise** a wonder **and**
bewilderment in Taurello, which resulted in the
latter's seeing that here was an instrument fitted
for his purposes, an engine powerful indeed when
set in motion, but utterly irresponsible, **and** which
could be made work in any direction **if only**
managed aright—let us once more recur **to the**
acknowledged necessity for Sordello and **his** people
that his development should be accomplished in
the way which actually happened ; and if we have
seen how nobly at the right moment Sordello forced
his egoism into alliance with **his** altruism, and
espoused the cause of humanity ; surely it is plain
that he was **no** irresponsible enthusiast. But it

may be worth while to consider shortly the reasons
for the obvious fact that Sordello was obscure in
his speech and mode of expressing his thoughts.

His nature, then, was, as has been shown
throughout, one in which perception was predomi-
nant. Instances abound through the poem to show
that if in his inmost mind he grasped a truth, he
never let it go. But, as must always be the case
where the will is greater than the power, the very
vigour with which his strong soul clutched the
truth in his bosom, made it the more difficult for
his weak bodily powers to free it from its imprison-
ment and display it to men. And since simple
truth, simple supremacy, will always seem complex
and obscure to low and double-dealing minds, it
was not the enervating influence of self-introspection, but the inborn vigour and earnestness of a
pure and supreme mind, which made Sordello's
utterances, straight from the fountain-head of truth,
seem incomprehensible to the dull ears of a man
whose life had been spent in double-dealing, in
striving after low ideals.

Although irresponsibility and fickleness of purpose in reality formed no part of Sordello's nature,
it may be well to deal finally with the last possible
objection, which implies the existence in him of·
these defects, by saying that when he was offered the

leadership of the Ghibellins, whom he was vowed to oppose, all his nature roused itself to force him to yield to this temptation, and only death saved him from the unutterable disgrace of passing his days as Taurello's tool and Palma's plaything.

But is it not true that Sordello's soul saw all things in the world by a clear light hidden from common men; and working steadily on by that light, refused to turn to the right hand or to the left from any clear shown truth? When once he was shown the claims of men as superior to the claims of himself, he never rested until he had spent himself in asserting those claims; when tempted by the kingdoms of the world and their glory, he yet steadily weighed in the balance the right against the wrong, the world against self, time against eternity. Is this man irresponsible because he is fervent, because he is unused to tricks of diplomacy, because he sees men's rights, once plainly put before him, with eyes undimned by self-interest? Let us judge him rather by that very agony which seemed to be his timely salvation from lasting disgrace. The nobility of his nature was to be keenly sensuous; the pride of his nature based itself in the royalty of his imagination; the strength of his nature pierced through the veil of morality to estimate truly the reason for the laws of right and wrong in this world. And when against these strong forces of his nature he brings to battle a force still mightier, the force of that stern sense of truth which will compel the bounties of his being into subjection to the round of duties which the world gives, when he binds these mighty forces together in harness like primeval monsters, to plough, and draw, and toil for the pigmies among whom they might have roamed spreading destruction, surely the divinity of his nature in the last fierce struggle asserts itself, and lets the broad-winged angel free to soar with plumes unworn, unstained, unshackled, towards the heaven which is its home!

SAUL.

THIS Lyric, besides possessing as a work of art many excellences which it would be beside my purpose to speak of here, has also beauties in its dramatic element which have arrested my attention. These beauties appeal strongly to the sympathies of any earnest thinker, and find a fit exponent and a full realisation in the collective mind of the strivers of to-day.

The poem details an intellectual battle of the highest order; the working of the imagination up to its highest pitch by means of the will, in order to produce a direct and visible effect upon another man. It is not, however, only because the actual motive of the poem is an interesting one, but because a certain quality of mind is displayed in one of the characters delineated—a quality of mind on which I shall at the end of this essay dwell with some minuteness—that the poem seems to me so important.

But before we enter into any examination of the thoughts arising out of the poem, let us first trace

the poem itself in a short explanation, and see
what are the effects, direct or indirect, of the
struggle of a man's intellect, as those effects are
drawn by the poet ; that struggle being, one must
assume for the present, an historical fact.

The dramatis personæ are, Saul king of Israel,
and David.

As Saul lay in one of those trances of melancholy which so often seized him, they sent for
David to come and sing with his harp, that by the
charm of his music he might 'cause the evil spirit
to depart from Saul.'

David came, and entered the tent where the
king hung, supported by his arms, on the cross-
beam which upheld its drapery.

How does David begin this terrible task, this
setting of brain to brain, in a battle more moment-
ous and more awful than the Goliah fight ?

Let us picture to ourselves the attitude of the
two men's minds.

Here are two human creatures; the one, sunk
far down out of the empyrean where life, the
chorægus, leads the chorus of humanity, to the
rhythm of a noiseless melody, in a perpetual dance
of dazzling light; and another who has stooped,
bidden by God, down from that empyrean, to
plunge into the black slough in which, too inert

and dead for any effort at escape, the lost man
wallows silently. From the utmost verge of that
black slough, from the far-away gate of hell at
which he lies, obstinately marrowless, so stupidly
negative that even hell's king scorns to open and
welcome him, who can bring him back? Can
David, so white and joyous, so glowing with the
life dance? Let us see.

He takes his harp, and begins to play a tune by
which he calls his sheep, when they must come up
to the folding at eventide.

Thus he calls to the wretch's mind that as the
sheep must follow their shepherd at the end of a
day, so must a man follow his shepherd Nature at
the end of a long sin. For a long sin ended in
lethargy is the end of a day in a man's intellectual
life; he has sucked out of that sin all the good
which is necessary to give him the lesson of life
which that sin is intended to teach; he has filled
himself full with the poison of it, which will soon
rack him with unutterable pain; the great fatalist
work is done for that time, and he must now come
quietly back, bearing within him the pasturing
of guilt, to the fold from whence he started; he
must come back to chew the cud of that terrible
meal, and let Nature do her work, and give him
her nourishment therefrom.

That tune seems **to** say, Anything is better
than deadness and inertia; come, sting yourself
with remorse, be awake, alive; **see the sin** you
have sinned and acknowledge it, and wrestle and
bruise, and beat yourself; you in **your** responsi-
bility and your pride are just as liable to Nature's
laws as the sheep are; they, **though** white and
untorn by bushes **of** error, meekly **obey** their shepherd; how **much** more then should **you**, so scarred
and wounded **by the** stresses of your long wander-
ings, **come home to be** folded, and healed, and
made clean!

And then, **even as** the sheep, the simplest **creatures, come** quietly **home, even so,** high above us,
at the **end of** *their* **day,** the stars, the creatures of
highest **mystery, come back quietly** to their home,
the sky. **All day long they have** pastured and
done their holy **unspeakable** office to millions, each
a greater **than you are; all day** long they have
been away, **and** their great pure fold has been
empty and **still; but now one** by one from the
distance they come gently **in,** faintly seen at first,
slowly brightening out **into** splendour, until the
whole mighty fold broods itself into an intense
purple blue, and its countless denizens lie sparkling
and singing in its bosom, penned **round by the
dark** colourless night.

But Saul hangs **motionless still**; his spirit will not come home at the call of the sheep's tune.

Then **David breaks into a new** melody; **that** which draws the quails after **him who plays, and** makes them leave each **his mate to follow the** player. The sound of it seems **to say to the lawless** monarch in grave rebuke; will **you not** acknowledge subjection to the law and the fold of the shepherd? will you madly insist that **you, a** wild untutored creature, are above all laws? Be **it** so! Yet even wild creatures are creatures still; Nature keeps secret spells in hidden places which shall draw **even** the wildest when she wills it; above and beyond all acknowledged law **is that** thing which we call the power of God, of which the utmost, terriblest force is never shown until a man is too far gone to acknowledge human laws.

Let Saul then beware; let him leave his mates **of melancholy** and black despair, and follow the strange sound and eerie light of which he knows not the cause, but **which** some inner impulse **of** his nature, also unreasoned out, bids him to follow. That hidden impulse, that secret law, are sternly existent, will you or no; and the two between them must draw and drive the sinning man; but let him once break from the one and avoid the other: and he must **drop** into the abyss from which comes no sound.

But still the spirit of the king is tranced and deaf.

And again David plays. He plays the tune which makes the crickets dance and fight; again he re-iterates in it the burden, God's law is above man's law; all human desires, all human or living sym-pathies, must bow in mute obedience to the great supremacy.

Then, for Saul still hangs stark and dumb, a gentler, stranger, tune comes stealing round him— a tune which speaks of pleading mercy; a tune which lulls the angry fiends who rage over the rapt and eyeless soul of the man, and yearns to make him hear (all in vain) how God, who can ruin and annihilate mountains and kingdoms, can also stoop and quietly stroke and soothe his tenderest, wist-fullest small creatures.

Beyond the reach of the voice which moves dumb creatures, Saul is mad indeed.

By the hopes and joys of human kind, by the whole of grace and majesty, let another effort be made for his deliverance.

The tune of the reapers. Shall it not picture to the king his own lowly subjects, never ashamed to show sympathy and good fellowship? shall not the warm exultant chords tell him of men who yearn for him, and are ready, nay eager, to stretch out hands and drag him from his quagmire? The tune of the dead man praised on his journey; shall not its solemn cadence, its passionate wail that rises to triumphant jubilance, call up the image of the love men bear to him who is gone, and the gentleness that forgets faults and shortcomings?

The marriage chant; the song that speaks of creation; shall not this thrill him with the thought of new men to be born, and endless blisses of wedded life? The battle song; shall not this rouse the king to stern fight with his inner enemies, and shake him once more into the old warriors' ardour?

No: the pageant of music wings its stately way past the spirit corpse: no motion shows returning life: silence falls.

But hark! In far recesses of his brain Saul hears a little, terrible sound, that swells and swells; upon his nerveless sense comes the throbbing rhythm of a solemn intoned chant; it is the chant of priests who go in set array into the presence of the very God.

Within his shut eyes, he seems to see the cloud, the splendour, which veil the face of the Judge whom he has contemned: the memory of the criminal awoke; and 'in the darkness, Saul groaned.'

David, wrestling in blind darkness with an unknown power, agonising for the mastery, catches a

gleam of light to direct his effort. He finds that
the deep subtle lessons taught through the dumb
animals, have had no effect; that the more obvious
lessons taught through human sympathy and suffering, have had no effect; but when the religious chord is touched, and in its vibration shakes
the heart with the mystery and the dreadness of
the hidden power, which ruled the Jews before
Saul ruled them, and itself created and anointed
him king; when the terror of these memories is
like to thrust the poor struggler yet further back
into the quaking slough, then David adroitly seizes
the slight indication of returning life and thought
which that groan of remorse showed, and strives to
throw to the choking man who has just recovered
consciousness in his struggle, a rope of joy. He
sings of the mad joy of simple vigorous life under
the sky, in the full health of a man; he sings of
Saul's boyhood and early days of soldiership; of
his piety and love for his parents; of his fellowship
with his brothers; of his early friendships, his early
aspirations, realised beyond all hope; of his kingship at last; of all the glorious things that his
kingship had wrought.

As the inner throes of the rock let free the gold
within it, so all the throes, the joys, and sorrows,
battles, rages, strengths, beauties, of his life, had

combined to one effort, to bring forth in **Saul** the golden spectacle of a God-nurtured king **who** should **conquer** and **be loved** by the world.

And now, at last, the **icy** barrier **which all** the **storms and** winds of subtle thought had **failed to move, tumbled,** and fell headlong **beneath** the **force of this** direct appeal to his own **life and** its **'fruits** hitherto in joy and strength, and his new opened eyes saw an image of future bliss and power. The icy barrier fell, even **as the** snow on the mountain's breast, having withstood all the storms and blasts of winter, falls down **before the first warm** breath of spring, and leaves **its bosom** naked **to the** touch of Nature and a loving **sun, to bring** forth under that touch new fruits of gracious kindness to all lowly and tender things.

There Saul stood, black, rent, and scarred by past **storms;** shall David's spirit have power, like the **breath of** spring upon the naked stone-breast of the mountain, to draw from Saul's stony breast **many** tender growths of returning life?

As the new spring, which has freed the mountain from its prisoning breastplate of snow, is not ashamed **to use** its old wiles of many centuries, its old experiences gathered from lowly lands, from little humble bare patches made fruitful, so David is not ashamed to **use** all **the** thoughts and fancies whereby in his mind, his own lowly patch of ground, he had raised little seedling herbs, which he meant should grow **and** flourish into great trees of knowledge and experience and love. As the spring uses the same grand secrets of nature on her greatest and lowliest forms, so David uses all the secrets which he had hitherto garnered, all the soft warm breaths of sympathy and knowledge in which his humble self had grown and rejoiced, to influence this lofty world-renowned man, the king of God.

Having seen from Saul's gesture, that though awakened **by his glowing** picture of the joy of physical living, **he yet** tacitly put aside such enjoyment as useless, **David takes** the path which leads **him to the** higher uses for **which** the physical life **is the schoolmaster and nurse.** He shows how Saul's life **from its infancy was** guarded through all its gracious **plenitude of joy, by** God's loving spirit, from harm **and sin; how like** a palm-tree his physical life had **grown,** broke into leaf, broke into bloom of strength, **beauty, and** manhood. You have done well, **says he, to see that** all this living, good though it has been hitherto to bring you to beauty **and** perfection, is **yet of no use** in itself, if before it bears any fruit, storms of sin and misfortune come over you, strip the leaves **and** flowers, and leave you nothing but a majestic **ruin. But** have you not

also, besides leaves and flowers, borne fruit? **Has**
not your life been full of fruit in your kingship?
True, this fruit seems to have been crushed **and**
trodden by your calamity and this terrible madness;
but what **of** that? Do not men crush the palm-fruit,
and out of its juice make a wine which comforts
and cures sorrow? Had it not been for nature's
tending hand which gently dandled the baby
sprout and gently brought up the young sapling
until it grew to a mighty tree, where would have
been the fruit which we must **crush before it** will
yield us the wine? Had it not been for **your long**
life which grew and bloomed unconsciously **to**
yourself into the full physical life of the man,
where would have been those fruits of kingship
which have been of some use even hitherto, and
must be of more use yet? Even as the wine comes
of crushing the fruit, so the good to be extracted
from the **fruits** of a man's life can only be extracted
by the crushing hand of suffering and sin. But,
while the fruit of the palm-tree would not have
come without the growth and beauty of the palm
itself, still sooner or later the palm itself must die,
while the store of wine from successive seasons of
date-harvest will last, to cheer and revive men for
many years. Even so, the life of the flesh which
produced your fruit, must fade one day; but the

wine which suffering has produced from that fruit
lasts, and keeps its strength and virtue. Again ;
each deed which you have done, like the palm-fruit,
is gathered in its ripeness; God the Husbandman
takes it, crushes it, seems to destroy it, but really
uses it to produce the wine of its good effect for the
use and comfort of men. Again ; as the winter
destroys the fruits of the summer, to make fresh
forms for the fresh year, so God destroys the effect
of your deeds, only to make, out of their decay and
ruin, new forms for new fruits. And again ; as the
sun does the good things, though sometimes tém-
pests and clouds will not let him see his work, nay
destroy that work ; even so, you have done the
good things, and though the clouds and tempests
of suffering and sin sometimes blind your eyes,
these will pass, and you will again behold your
deeds breaking out into new flowers of beauty and
use. Then use all that you have done, all that
you will do, and shine over it with benignant rays
of sympathy, to make each little action bear fruit
a hundred-fold.

But if unlike the sun, throned high for countless
years, your graciousness and strength and beauty
fade and fall, you can yet take a new use for age,
and look forward. You can foresee that your
deeds which were only seeds and shrubs when you

looked on them as **past** things, will in a far-off future become stately **trees**; **you can** foresee **all** the glory **and praise which** men **will** heap **upon** your good actions, till they culminate in the **in-destructible** monument **of** your trust, **your grey tomb of** marble heaped four square, on **whose face is cut in** great characters the story of all your fame.

Thus did David, in the strife of prayer, lift Saul's **soul out of** the darkness into the light of life. Thus did **he at** last draw the huge bulk up from the paralysing grasp of the slough snake which **had** encircled **him.** Saul, a man once **more,** was come back to the world, with **a new light of wonderful** love in his face.

Then out **of** the unconscious yearning which **had** prompted that mighty effort of David's, **out** of that **prayer** spirit which had sustained him hitherto, there **arose** to help David, in yet another prophetic flight, **a** yearning too divine to be borne.

Music and **harp** were useless now; he **must** use the great irrepressible man-love which welled up in him for music, and say all his say out with the full heart which **is** greater than **all** beauty of sight and sound. Scarcely knowing how **to use** the pile of knowledge **he** has gathered, he **turns** to review all **that he has said, in** order that if possible by his **past** experience he may learn **how** to use his love.

'I have spoken and judged of all God's creation: and on every hand, beneath the stress of my agony of prayer, untold depths have opened themselves, all tending to one deeper abyss of knowledge withheld. In the glow of the Goodness of Creation, I stand aware of my own nothingness, confounded, shrivelled, by God's perfection. Yet, though I cower so low, I fail not to see, in every one of God's creatures, some special attribute. I tremble, but ask, shall not I, God's creature too, find in myself some such attribute? Looking fearfully into myself, I find that attribute in the motive which impelled me to this task of prayer and prophecy. It was love of God, love of man, love of the king whom I desire to rescue. But finding this attribute, I shrink back appalled from it. In the whole mass of creation, in this very ruin of a king, I see the work of Power. Shall I, the creature, dare to show this my love against God's power, triumph over God and his other creatures because they have it not? Dare I do this? Surely I dare and will! For in thus boasting of my power of love, do I not boast of a thing God has created in me, greater than all the rest? If all the other creatures are only feeble types of their Creator in his different parts, shall not this love of mine, great and overwhelming as it seems, be a feeble type only of

God's overwhelming love? Look again! I who would make Saul great, wise, and famous, cannot do it. It is but a desire, it is too only a creation in me by God. Had it been my own creation, my power would have equalled my will. I should surely have given all good things, and then, having given them, crown the gifts with the redeeming of Saul from ruin. But now, I can only imagine, and fall back powerless to achieve. Why then do I not despair for Saul? Because I feel and know that my desire to do, shows the germ of the power to do, at present weak and clogged by the mortal flesh. But since there is the germ, I know also that, like everything else which God has made, it is only the feeble finite type of an infinite attribute of God; that my weak unable desire and love are types of God's all-powerful, all-consummating love. And again; as my love is a type of and has its origin in God's love, is not my weakness a type of, has it not origin in, God's weakness too? Surely, as God has infinite power to love, so has he infinite weakness, and power therefore to be beloved. As surely as He, infinitely the strongest, shall bear the heaviest burden, so surely shall he, infinitely the weakest, sink beneath that burden below all human weakness, and from its depths rise up to pity and redeem mankind.

'O Saul, it shall be
A Face like my face that receives thee ; a Man like to me
Thou shalt love and be loved by, for ever ; a Hand like this
    hand
Shall throw open the gates of new life to thee ; See the Christ
    stand !'

So ends the superb prophecy which David's
agony produces from his lips.

And now, let us examine into the springs, the
forces, which the poet seems to imagine prompted
this wondrous rhapsody, and see what mood of
mind it dramatically shadows forth.

It has plainly then its foundation in transcendent-
alism, developed from the simple type of worship
of bygone ages, and is just as much a human
attribute as any other form of intellect developed.

What the attribute of mind is, which produced
these wonderful effects, what use that attribute has
had, still has, and will have, as a power in working
the world, it will be our business to enquire.

It appears then that the attribute of mind which
was the moving force in the struggle of David's
intellect with Saul's madness as described in the
poem, is one which must be called the spirit of
prayer.

Now at present I shall do no more towards
explanation of this phrase, 'spirit of prayer,' than
call attention to the fact that it impliedly relates

to what is usually called the religious element in
man's nature, and that it would **appear to have**
been handed down from man to man of a particular
race. I say thus much in order to draw attention
to the quarter whence the train of thought will be
pursued. This quarter is Palestine, Canaan, the
early ground of that religion of **the Jews which**
David held, which was the father of Christianity,
and **as** such author of the highest civilisation.
Having indicated the nature of the proposed examination so far, I should observe (just to remove
all doubt as to the tendency of the discussion), **that**
in dealing with the subject **of** this spirit of prayer
it would be plainly useless and **beside the** purpose
to speak of prayer either from the point of view of
any religion which has existed or does exist; or,
of any special system of prayer, as such, created
by **any** religionists; or even of the question of the
efficacy or inefficacy of praying to God; because
any **one** of these subjects would lead only to
endless branchwork of theological **discussion**;
because what we have to do is to examine into a
particular attribute of a particular Jew, but an
attribute shared in different degrees by Jew and
Greek, bondsman and freeman, white and black.

Having thus hitherto only stated nakedly what
seems to have been the force which impelled David

in the foregoing poem to this work of resuscitating
Saul; having called that force the spirit of prayer;
and having also implied that David was only one
of a series in a great chain of people, whose influence (through this spirit of prayer, as will hereafter appear,) has been by far the most important
influence of any which has worked in civilising the
world from the earliest times to the present; it is
obviously necessary to go back as far as history
will carry us, and trace the stream of that people
from its source. And since the spirit of prayer
had its development in what we may call the
primitive religion of that people; and in order to
trace its cause, and see clearly its ultimate effect
on the civilised world, we must examine into the
beginning of that religion. How far back must we
go to look for the beginning of this religion? We
must go back to the first man who founded the
Jews, the author of that religion; and trace upwards from him through his descendants.

The plan of the examination will, therefore, resolve itself into something like this form. We
shall be dealing with the history of a religion which
has produced the type (shown forth in the Jewish
and Christian, Old and New, Testaments), which is
admitted to be the highest existing type of God.
It is from the Old and New Testaments that we

naturally select five chief men, in whose history may fairly be traced the **birth** and growth of the spirit of prayer. We shall consider the nature of that quality, **and** note how, **in** greater or less degree, it would seem to exist still, and to be very often called into exercise, in every earnest man's life ; we shall see what it has done, in and through **those** five Jews, as exemplified in the main points **of** their history; and from these conclusions we shall deduce **its** importance as **a** ruling force in every work.

Taking, therefore, the historical facts of the Old and New Testaments as a groundwork, **Abraham,** Jacob, Moses, David, and Jesus, seem **to be the** five chief men who were the strongholds **of this** important attribute. Because these five characters seem, through the overpowering force of the prayer spirit **in them, to** have been the primal **engine in** making **the** highest religions of the world ; **and** because **those** religions have been the **ruling influence** which **has** made the civilisation of **the world** what it is, there seems small apology needed for treating of their dominant characteristic with some minuteness, in tracing it up to **the point** of David's struggle as described in the **poem, and** downward from that point to the present time.

Of Abraham, **whose** life is niggardly doled to us

in twelve short pages, one feels almost awe in speaking, at this far away time, when the simple men of past ages loom giant-like through a mist of centuries.

He is the first worshipper; a man who stands up before us for a moment, in the sudden blaze out of the darkness of those early times, as one to whom ' God had said.'

The very first historical fact recorded of him shows us the existence in him of some innate yearning which moved him where other men were quiet, and lights up his image around the undistinguishable grey ghosts of the past. It grew and burned in him as he lived an uneventful life among placid pastoral tribes, until at last, consumed by the resistless force of it, he left his native country, to work out a life for himself. He became rich in flocks and herds, a king among shepherds; he developed and forged by the heat of that fire, qualities unknown among his peaceful compatriots; and was soldierly, unscrupulous, and yet honourable; superstitious, and yet coolheaded; stern, yet kind and hospitable. But what distinguished him above all his contemporaries was, not any one of these qualities, which doubtless had representatives in obscurer men, but the fire by which he forged his manhood and his sovereignty, the yearning in him

which was the spirit of prayer. It was his religion
(call it superstition if you will), which was the real
force to make him great. A religion which displayed itself in the building of altars, in the seeing
of visions, in curious self-thwartings; a religion
which was the visible effect of the prayer spirit's
domination. Paradoxical man as Abraham surely
was, his contradictions did not thwart his purpose,
for they were welded into intensified force by the
ruling fire.

Perhaps in spite of, and perhaps because of his
paradoxes, at any rate by virtue of his blooming
sensuousness, he ruled his fellows, and took his
own way. But above and beyond his qualities,
great as they were, the quivering wings of the
prayer spirit lifted him; wife and nephew, sovereignty and riches, spoils and concubines, were to
him only as means to an end; every day was an
agonising step towards the prize on which he had
staked his life; and every act, kind or cruel, was a
result of his own aspiration; to the world he was
the mighty shepherd, and the kindly friend; to
himself he was none of these.

What was he, then, to himself? what was his
object? what seemed his failure? To be the father
of many nations; to be the man in whom all
families of the earth should be blessed; for these

things he lived and died; of these things in his life
and till his death he realised nothing, save that in
the dreary evening of his life, when pleasure was
gone from him, he had one son who was to be the
vessel in which the sacred fire should be kept safe.

That son, Isaac, does not appear in any way to
have exhibited in himself the qualities which show
the existence of the spirit of prayer. It is Jacob,
the younger of his twins, whose actions show that
he was the next recipient of the fire which had
slept since Abraham's death. It is curious that
this spirit of their great ancestor was so unequally
divided between Esau, the hairy fool, and Jacob,
his magnificent brother; but we are compelled by
the issue to believe that the world would not have
been what it is had they showed that spirit equally;
and the consequence, at any rate is, that while
Esau is represented by obscure tribes, who are no
further in the world than he was, when he fooled
away his birthright, any man in this nineteenth
century may be proud if he be, in his greatest
mental attributes, a representative of Jacob.

The singular union in Jacob of a perfidy and
hardness which had no place in Abraham, with a
religious fervour which exceeded Abraham's, and
with a fixity of purpose in satisfying his passion
for Rachel, which has become a model for all

lovers of women to this day; these characteristics
are here noticeable only for showing that all his
acts and thoughts, notably perfidious, calculating,
passionate, or devotional, were prompted by the
spirit of prayer, which made him the man he was.
Witness his dealings with Esau, Isaac, and Laban.
For what did he trick the great hunter, hoodwink
his father, and overreach his uncle? He bought
the birthright for a mess of pottage, because of his
firm conviction that he was, or his determination
to become, the prince of nations; he laid secret
and violent hands on his father's blessing, because
his superstition told him this was a necessary means
to that end; he baffled the cheating of Laban with
greater cunning, that he might still keep his supremacy, and be thereafter great; and all these, because his eyes were ever fixed on the same shining
goal. His purpose, seething in his brain, troubled
his sleep beneath the stars, made him a poet for
the nonce, and created the ravishing dream of the
Angels' ladder; his purpose, still triumphant in his
egoism, wrestled with him as Jehovah in his dis-
torted fancy, and named him Israel, a Prince with
God; his purpose, lighting up the dying embers
of his brain, drove him, by a singular foresight, to
bless Ephraim above Manasseh; and yet of its
fulfilment we can record only this; that though his

life, like Abraham's, was one bitter struggle for the fruition of Abraham's dream, he died far away from the land he was to people and to rule ; and though he saw children and children's children, could only spend his last breath in a wild prophecy of what, in times as far away as evening clouds, should yet be the triumphant end of all.

The historical steps which lead us from Jacob to the next standpoint on which the spirit of prayer displayed itself, are easy and plainly marked. Through many years of adversity his descendants grew to a great but oppressed people ; and when the time was come for the concentration of the fire in one man, that man arose with a new purpose, as plainly a sequence and development of that which Abraham lived for, as if he had actually spoken it in words to his far-away descendant. The well-known character of Moses shows for itself, without explanation, that to him we must look for evidence of the existence of the spirit of prayer in one man above all others for the time being. See how his generalship, statesmanship, and energy combined themselves with the prayer spirit, and lifted him far above either of his predecessors in its enjoy-ment ; and while it gave his life a greater import-ance, embittered his death with a more cruel pang. Alone, and by virtue of the prayer spirit, he roused

the sleeping passions of the great slave **nation ;**—
alone, and by dexterous arrangement of Pharaoh's
brutality, cowardice, and **cupidity, he so** intrigued
that the very elements seemed weapons **of a** per-
sonal God wielded in defence **of a** (so-called)
chosen people against the **Godless** Egyptians.
Alone, by force of that prayer spirit, he dragged
the fierce thousands through deserts, fiery serpents,
scorpions, plagues, and **death, to** Abraham's **land,**
crowded with terrible peoples who had been Abraham's friends; alone, through **the** prayer **spirit,**
among awful mountains, in fasting and privations,
he lived out, and declared as the words **of God, the**
law which has been the moral **code of all time,**
and which he made the Hebrews believe was the
very utterance, the very handgraving, on God-
created tables, of the invisible Jehovah ; and alone,
by force of the prayer spirit, he towered above the
people as **the** Viceregent of that Jehovah, through
communion with whom he seemed to rule the
waters and the plagues. And now, what an end
was his! The prayer spirit, which gave him his
wondrous personal influence on **his** people, was
hourly consuming **him ;** he never forgot his power
to the last ; **he** seemed in full sight, and almost
touch, **of** his purpose. But when the fire had
burnt him through and through ; and when at last,

his rage for once overcoming him, the wearied
flesh gradually sank beneath its wasting embrace.;
out of the emotion kindled by the superstition still
inwoven with his Godhead, he cursed himself for
disobedience to his self-created Deity, and the
bitter end of his dream was, with the last ebb of
strength to crawl to the top of Pisgah, and to die
in very sight of the cruel happy country, which
had slipped from his touch—for ever.   Oh, bitter
last minutes of the man's life!   To have toiled and
thought, intrigued, prayed, and believed ; to have
used the thunder as his own, and drawn the
people like one man with the fiction of the God-
graven tables ; to have lain tranced in catalepsy
before the sapphire pavement, and come down
with glorified face to the grovelling Hebrews ; to
have brought the people home to fulfil Abraham's
dream, with power and laws of which Abraham
never dreamed ; and at the end—to die a worn-
out old man, at the very threshold of a paradise
which the sheep he had folded, leaving his clay
behind, would taste to the full!   If this is not
failure, where is failure ?   But again, if this is not
mightiest success, where has success ever been
proved ?

After Moses' death, the prayer spirit seems not
exactly to have slept, but to have become diffused

among the whole people whom Moses left so **sor-
rowfully**. Until **it narrowed again, to burn through**
the blue **eyes and in** the golden hair of that gracious
boy whose prophetic force **was the** subject of the
poem that has suggested **this train of** thought, **and
whom it** is fit that we should consider not only in
connection with the actual incidents of the poem,
but in those acts of his life which led up to those
incidents, and were afterwards such a result of
them as gave him the name in his own nation, nay,
among many thousands since, of the earthly father
of the Creator of the purest **of** all religions.

But at this point let us pause, and **assure ourselves that in** going so far back, **and** dwelling **so**
minutely on the lives of David's forefathers, **we
have** not wandered from our subject. What have
these details of the lives of Abraham, Jacob, and
Moses, to do with the one struggle of David's
spirit which is the avowed theme of **the** poem?
The connection is not far to seek. Abraham's
dream, at Jacob's death, was far nearer fulfilment
than it was at his own death, and far nearer fulfilment at Moses' death than **it** was at Jacob's.
Jacob saw a small tribe; **Moses** saw a mighty
nation. But even Moses saw only a mighty nation
just entering a strange land, **to do** inevitable battle
with mightier men, the dwellers in that land. It

was many years, and there were many reverses and
successes, before the Jews were great enough to set
up for themselves a king ; but not until they had
done so, did David begin to breathe, or, at any
rate, to think.   Abraham's dream, which began in
his own bosom, was, in David's time, a household
word in the mouth of every Jew ; Abraham's spirit
of prayer, by force of nationality, circumstances,
and social contact, had grown into a sacred flame,
kept as patriotically and earnestly as any nation
ever kept its visible symbols of nationality. David,
a poet from his birth, nursed in Nature's softest
lying, had created for the Jews, and for himself,
out of the traditions handed down from Abraham,
a glorious future far greater than Abraham could
ever imagine ; in him the yearning which begun in
Abraham's breast was fanned to a glow by the
wings of many hundred years. If, then, it was his
desire, as it had been that of Abraham, Jacob, and
Moses, to help the great people on their march
through Time, have we not abundant reason why
he should thus strive to rouse Saul, the head of
that people into burning life, lest the body should
fall lifeless and become a prey to the birds and
beasts who were thronging around it ? And looking at his whole life, before and after he strove for
Saul, is not the prayer spirit manifest in him ?

That he was and is the great poet of religion; that the influence of his acts **which it impelled,** the wild words it made him write, nay the very' failures and crimes in which it involved him, added **to the acts of Abraham,** Jacob, and Moses, were the ground-work of many of the rhapsodies called prophecy, **and were** and are the force which helped **on** the **great Jewish** and Christian religions, all these con-sequences resulted from the working in his mind, during his shepherd life, of the supreme spirit **of** prayer.

That spirit, which roused **Saul as we have seen,** burned brightly during the bandit life into which David was forced by Saul's gloomy suspicion; he thought always **and** supremely of the Jews as a people; and when' Saul at last fell, he hesitated **not for** a moment to step into the throne whence **his brain** could help his people on their great journey.

Fusing into **a** glowing mass all the heaped up traditions of his life from Abraham downwards, the prayer spirit gradually melted out in his brain an image which was to be the idol **of** his life. For his *hope* was that he should **be** the instrument through whom Abraham's ideal should be realised; **that** he should become, as **he** did become, the **King** of the Hebrews, and lead them up to and set them upon a pinnacle of glory high over other nations.

But, again, his *ideal* was, that he should do more than these things; the very highest pinnacle of his dream palace was, having lifted the people thus, to show the world what homage the greatest people could pay to their greatest God in a temple made with hands.

Of this dream he never lost sight. It was with him as the robber chief, among mountains, fast-nesses, and shaking perils; it enfolded him when he took Saul's life in his hand, and dropped it back safe in the sleeping owner's breast; it lifted him when he charmed away the giant king's madness with his simple harp songs; it fired him when he killed the messenger who told him of Saul's death; and when he took his throne, and with sure strong feet crushed out the last sparks of rebellion, still his eyes were lit up with its glory. Nay, when his place was safe, and all men bowed to the warrior and the king, even then he never forgot. The people waxed greater and greater beneath him; he was the terror of his world; he had concubines, wives, children; but his ideal never came. He had been a man of blood; and his stained hands might not do for his God the work for which he had spent his life. When he learned in his arrogance that he

numbered near a million of fighting men, the pes-
tilence withered his pride; his darling child drove
him from his throne; while his mightiest son was
to surpass him in splendour, the crowning sin that
produced that son thrust David beneath the feet of
his own servant; and he died worn out, with shouts
of rebellion ringing in his ears.

The traditions of Abraham, Jacob, Moses, and
David were, many hundred years after David's
death, the life of every Hebrew, man, woman, and
child; they had gathered enormous power under
the wild times of the captivity, from the fervid
prophet odes, under the rod of the oppressor: but
the times were dark; the glory was departed; the
real Lord of the world had set his foot upon them;
there seemed nothing left but to wait, hope, and
prophesy.

The prayer spirit which had burned in David's
Hebrews, paling as they rose, and brightening with
their fall, towered into a star, and descended with
the added heat of centuries of passion, among
solemn-eyed oxen, into a poor struggling baby,
lying in a manger. That night is still wrapped in
a weird solemnity of Godhead; for the greatest of all
men who held the prayer spirit, had begun to live.

Greater than Abraham; simpler than Jacob;
humbler and stronger than Moses; purer than

David; his ideal was clearer and higher than theirs, his failure more complete.

Not more than a dozen people knew or cared that he was born; he was scoffed at when he first rose to preach; his very miracles (so called) brought him into great peril; and only the lowest of his people loved him. But when other boys were children, he was a man; he set himself to redeem his people from the Romans; to be pure himself; to make them pure; to make them the greatest people.

And oh! maddest and sweetest of dreams, he dreamed that he was God's son, and very God; and he set himself to make the world believe it. This was the deep well-spring of his actions, this carried him through his cruel life; this supported him in the pangs of death.

Always gentle and uncomplaining; always tired, but never wearied, he knew and could do such things as the light of superstition and love in those simple times brightened into miracles. He was never giddy at the height to which homage raised him, and his life is undimmed by a single cloud of anger, impurity, or excess.

But the naked torture in whose gripe he sank, would have been a cruel vengeance on the vilest robber; and thus let us seal the last page in the history of the King of Worshippers, lest we blot it with our tears.

Now in the exercise of the spirit of prayer in these five men, which was the moving power in the things they did, which is in greater or less degree existent in every man, and is called into exercise in most days of every man's life, there was, we see, one necessity or fate; every one of them failed in the thing he had to do. Failure was all their dower, failure which was to become success in some future age.

What, then, is it which makes this spirit of prayer so important, if failure is a necessity of its exercise? To ascertain this, we must now examine into the nature of the attribute, and gather from our story what it has done.

We are to consider that particular quality of mind, or, perhaps, it would be more correct to say that particular point in their upward struggle, to which all men's minds do at some time attain, (a point which with reference to the particular mind is the same, but in minds with reference to each other is higher or lower according to relative strength or weakness,) which results in, or actually is, Prayer.

The spirit of prayer then is a quality which, when it possesses a man, gives to him as an attribute the necessity of looking and hoping beyond his sight; makes him create for himself at once, more or less distinctly and personally, and in the teeth of his reason, a God to whom he can cry; makes, and has made, all existing ideas of God. Further, the spirit of prayer imperiously drives its possessor to spend his whole force in doing or getting something far beyond his reach; it so drives him, till he falls nerveless on the ground, crying for very weakness, 'my muscles are flesh, not iron;' having so driven and thrown him, it works through and through every fibre in his nature, and while he grovels and screams for help, tells him — as a triumphant climax, and in the topmost ecstasy of his agony—that in the darkness stands a formless thing, a shrouded power, his God in fact, who will now or hereafter do or get for him the thing he desires; and that what now seems the awfullest failure shall shine as the mightiest success.

It is not hard to exemplify this definition in the five men whom we have been considering, and to show what has been achieved through their exercise of the spirit of prayer.

Of Abraham, it seems scarcely too much to say, that in virtue of the ideal which he set up, and which was created in him by the prayer spirit, he is what he dreamed to be—the man in whom all families of the earth are blessed. Why? First,

because that spirit, which bore him through life
resistless, though it threw him fainting in darkness
at the end, where no ray showed the glory which
was to be, and which he had conceived, has, joined
with the acts of Abraham's life, been a living influence in every Jew since his time, and has thus
swayed the fortunes of the civilised world from his
time to our own. And, again, it is not only in the
realisation of his hopes that the spirit of prayer has
had its fruit. For the very reason that Abraham
could propose to himself an object so far beyond him,
so impossible for him to realise; for the very reason
that for a seeming hopeless end, which was to result
beyond and above his hopes, in the making of the
civilised world, he spent his force, and so far as he
could see, failed and fell—for this very reason, and
not because his dream has come truer than his
maddest hopes could conceive, but out of the very
cause of his agony, and in virtue of his failure—he
is throned above in our thoughts as a chief among
worshippers, as one of the men who have striven
earnestly.

So, with Jacob and Moses, in whom was produced, with sustained, but greater intensity, the
prayer spirit of Abraham with all its consequences.
Both men kept in view Abraham's ideal, glorified
by images made out of their own individuality; but,

while both seemed to see more of their triumph, their failure was to themselves as bitter as the others.

Their superstition was dominant, and as intimately woven in with the prayer spirit as that of Abraham; but this last was intensified in them, both by the fact of their being eaten through with the tradition of their forefathers, that the race of Abraham should rule the world, and from the acquired vigour of growth and circumstances.

And in Jacob and Moses was not their failure a success? Was it not because of that failure, and the necessity for ultimate fulfilment, that the prayer spirit which burned in them was kept alive in their children, till it drove them back to Canaan? Did it not make them a great people, dictate the great moral law, and to say it once more, help to make us what we are?

And tracing the immediate effects of the spirit of prayer as shown in the immediate successors of Moses, it is fair to say, that David would not have been what he was, done what he did, had it not been for the spirit of Moses descended to him. David, shepherd, warrior, and king; David, the concentration of Abraham's fire; what have we seen was the issue of *his* life? Not once did the prayer spirit forsake him; through his cruelty and crime, his losses and successes, it up-

held him. In him far more than in his predecessors
the spirit of prayer asserted **its** power; for it was
through **the use he** made **of it** in his remorse for
his blackest crime that he was able to train up a
son who **should** fulfil his ancestor's desires, be
cherished by his subjects, and known in worlds of
which David had never heard. **It** was because of
the use that he made of the spirit of prayer that
his songs have lived till now, that he was for centuries the pattern for great kings. Last and highest
of all, he was, though he never knew it, the direct
ancestor of the man who for nearly 2000 years has
been worshipped as the Son **of** God himself. Yet
I have shown how he too, like the rest, failed utterly
in comparison with his desires; how pleasure went
from him and **he** died a wreck.

    Jesus of Nazareth has created a firm belief of
his Godship, **not** only **in** his immediate followers,
but **in a large** part of the world. Through the
force **of** the prayer spirit, he ruled all who ap-
proached him; founded and has maintained a
moral code **which** vivifies that of Moses, and
will be remembered when Moses is forgotten.
—Through the worship of Jesus men have been
humanised; the worship of Jesus has been through-
out the world's history the strongest engine of
power.—Yet in **his** life, more than in all the others

put together, is exemplified the truth laid down,
that although what seemed the awfullest failure
then should shine hereafter as the mightiest success, failure at the time of strife is a necessity of
the spirit of prayer.

To sum up all that has been said, let us remember that the prayer spirit has never been inde-
pendently in any one of those five men, but has
derived its added force from the knowledge of
what some one else has done; that, be this as it
may, the prayer spirit is still an attribute which
each of those five men, had they consented to be
guided by their reason, would have made it their
life's business to crush; but that, since the prayer
spirit (which you may call, if you will, credulity,
superstition, or fanaticism) triumphed over reason,
the victory has made its subjects both princes and
saviours.

And, again, let us notice that only when these
men were so wrought with fire that they were
carried thereby to the school of their weakness, to
a confession of the possible veiled power, only then
and at that point did they pray; only as they
possessed and cherished in themselves the God-
begotten necessity of striving thus madly, and
could believe that in failing thus utterly they did
in truth triumph, has their work lived till now, and
with it live hereafter.

Having seen, then, **how** the prayer spirit domi-
nated all the five men described, how its force
created each ideal; **how that** ideal first failed, then
succeeded: how triumphant has been Abraham's
ideal in the worship of Jesus—let us see **in a few**
words what the prayer spirit, handed down through
generations from those five men, has done.

The concentration of purpose, the absolute piti-
lessness, with which all of them worked to their
end; these strong weapons, used perpetually **on**
the men around them, hewed out some part of the
fabric which was to be built, and **cowed and de-**
stroyed all opposers, sooner **or later.**

Always, the fact of any man's **having had one**
burning idea throughout his life will communicate
some of his fire to some successors ; this contagion
spreads, the idea gains countless forces on its side,
and nations make a pride **of** some thought or
scheme, which single great men were scoffed **at or**
killed for entertaining.

Although, **at** this day, no man does what the
old Jews did for **a** religion or an **idea** like Abraham's, the principle which moves a man now in
any research or purpose, scientific, political, artistic
—what you will—is nothing more or less than the
spirit of prayer.

Had it not been **for the** Jews, Christianity would

T

not have been: had it not been for Christianity, civilisation as it now exists would not have been. Civilisation would have been as nothing had not the same spirit, which made Abraham and his successors erect a God for our worship, urged the great men of Europe in the cause of the world and the men in it.

Surely, then, it is not hard to see how the spirit of prayer has influenced every great modern work, how every great man's life is yet instinct with the fire of it; not hard to see how the conception of which a man can achieve only the millionth part, is reverently taken up by man after man, until the toil of ages triumphantly completes it amid the silent prostration of the world.

And now, even now, the prayer spirit is neither dead nor dumb; it struggles and burns in you and me; it dominates Nature.

And it is in the sound of the wind; it wakes in the buds of spring; it leans from the yearning of an evening sky; it vibrates in the magical promise of the morning.

The cry of a dog is eloquent of prayer; the horses' nostril quivers with it; every line in a man's worn face, every knot in a man's rugged hand, is the trace of a bygone prayer.

By it, man is most human, for he only feels

beyond his sight, he only desires what he cannot see : by it, man is most godlike, for he only is lifted, through his sense, by his desires, to the kingdom where the veil is rent in twain.

When we want, though we use no words, we pray the more passionately in dumb entreaty, and set our muscles anew to get our desire ; and though we do not get it, the world, and we, are better for the strife.

Through the spirit of prayer, Abraham, Jacob, Moses, and David, still live ; and when the religion of Jesus has passed away, men will remember the dream-life of the Hebrew carpenter, and the blessed consequences of following out the maddest and noblest of ideals.

Such are some of the thoughts which the poem of 'Saul' has awakened ; such are some of the conclusions to which a loving consideration of the thoughts in that poem have led me irresistibly.

We have dwelt at some length on the attribute which seems to have been in the poet's mind when he wrote the poem, and we have traced the course of that attribute from the beginning of David's people to David himself, and thence down to the present time.

Having thus dwelt, as fully as is possible in an essay like this, on the history of the spirit of prayer, let us turn once more to the subject of the poem itself, and see not only how that is an example of the exercise of the attribute, but also what direct thoughts, what actual lessons for ourselves, the poet desired to place before us.

It is plain that David, as drawn in the poem, fulfilled, in the intensity of his mental struggle, all the conditions of the spirit of prayer: that he was striving after an end which was not within the grasp of humanity; that he was drawn by it far beyond his first desire into regions of prophecy, and into the splendour of an idea which has ruled thousands for so many years—the idea of Christianity.

We see, too, that at the time when he crawled out of the tent, utterly exhausted, none of these splendours blest his eyes in their accomplishment; for it was not in his life, but hundreds of years after, that this idea was fulfilled.

But we see also that here the spirit of prayer had a particular field to work in, very different from the wide fields in which it ranged when David's forefathers and successors held it.

Here was no founding of a nation, or establishing a religion; nothing to win applause of a whole world. It was merely the work of one man upon another, a work prompted by the welling up of human love which, thank God, exists to-day as it did then.

For us of to-day, then, what is the lesson which the poet would teach ?

He surely says to us something like this : In this strife of David's, is there no warning for modern men ? Does not our work lie among each other? Are there not Sauls enough among us, whose temptations and madnesses, if they lack the gloom or glow of historical majesty, are only too plainly seen in their hideous reality? Surely every one of us may one day be a Saul, and let none triumph because he is hitherto spotless; and in the thought of this terrible possibility, let us each try and gather strength to become Davids upon fit occasion.

Let us, in plain words, admit that the duty of every man towards his fellows is, first to keep that sympathetic power at its fullest pitch, which enables him at any moment to bring a kind of mesmeric force to bear on any man who may need the aid of another's mind to expel some of the devils of the world or the flesh. The poem seems to teach us that it is this principle of direct influence over men which produces all the great works : that no man can attain perfection in that influence until he has first made his own life true at least, if not

pure also. And when that is done, it matters
little, surely, whether his influence be exercised
over six men or six millions, so long as the best is
done that can be done. The force is existent, and
redoubles itself in every new mind which sucks it
in; the force lives, and has more than ample
material, during one short life, in the changes and
chances which six most uneventful lives may bring
about, to work its possessor to the full agony of
the spirit of prayer; once the force is born, it is a
living thing whereby the world is moved; and
while it should be enough for any one man to die
feeling that his best is done, it is scarcely unreasonable to say that, although the fruit may
never be seen beyond the six men during its
owner's life, any effort truly directed, may, like the
efforts of Abraham, David, and Jesus, directly or
indirectly be the very instrument which makes a
nation, founds a kingdom, or establishes a religion.

THE DIGRESSION IN 'SORDELLO.'

AT the end of the Third Book of 'Sordello,' the
poet breaks off the thread of his story to enter into
a long digression, which while singularly obscure
in expression, is a remarkable, and of its kind
unique effort, in the direction of showing what are
the poet's views of the duties of his own class
towards mankind. This digression I have not
thought it well to speak of in its place in the
poem, lest the continuity in the interpretation of
the actual story should be disturbed. But the
ideas put forward by the poet on behalf of himself
and his fellows are so valuable, that it seems right,
after having dwelt with some care on the various
trains of thought whereby the poet was prompted
in writing the poems on which the foregoing essays
were written, to give as clearly as possible an explanation of the views expressed in this digression.

It will be remembered that the Third Book completes the first circle of Sordello's life, and brings
him within reach of his first ideal of making men

act out their faculties, by his influence. The poet
at this point of the story lets fall the curtain for
awhile, and—in order to account to the world for
his motive in writing the poem,—pursues a thread
of his own inner life.

He begins by laying it down as a principle, that
in all true works (such as he hopes this is) some
proofs escape to show that the singer is not giving
us the whole of his inner life and hope.   Underlying
such works, some thought like this seems to be in
the singer's mind: 'My life began before and will
continue after this work; although you may think
this subject engrosses my whole mind, it is not so;
I shall go my way, and leave that subject behind
me, perhaps never to take it up again.   But do not
imagine that because when my work on that subject is finished I have ceased to live in thought.
You may indeed mourn' because I continue silent,
you may perhaps complain of me for not giving
you the result of the deeper thoughts which did
underlie that work, and which I pursue and shall
pursue when that work is finished. You may
accuse me of inconstancy, in not remaining with
you (as the tone of my work seemed to promise I
would), to dwell with you for ever upon the subject;
you may perhaps complain that I, though professing
deep contemplation, do not give you nearly all the

result of it; that I never lay before you the scheme, the aspirations, of my whole life. But what then? My business first is to live my life out, not to speak of it; I must gather experience before I can impart it. If indeed an idea chains me down for a time, and works within me until the fire is kindled.and I am obliged to speak, then you have the benefit of my speech; but as soon as I have spoken it I must go away from you to gather fresh thoughts. I cannot stay and brood over this one thought for ever with you. To use a simile:

> 'Tis but a sailor's promise, weatherbound :
> ' Strike sail, slip cable, here the bark be moored
> For once, the awning stretched, the poles assured!
> Noontide above: except the wave's crisp dash,
> Or buzz of colibri, or tortoise' splash,
> The margin's silent : out with every spoil
> Made in our tracking—coil by mighty coil—
> This serpent of a river to his head
> I' the midst! Admire each treasure, as we spread
> The bank, to help us tell our history
> Aright : give ear, endeavour to descry
> The groves of giant rushes, how they grew
> Like demons' endlong tresses we sailed through :
> What mountains yawned, forests to give us vent
> Opened, each doleful side, yet on we went
> Till . . . may that beetle (shake your cap) attest
> The springing of a land-wind from the west! '
> ' Wherefore? Ah, yes, you frolic it to-day!
> To-morrow, and the pageant's moved away

> Down to the poorest tent-pole : we and you
> Part company : no other way pursue
> Eastward your voyage, be informed what fate
> Intends, if triumph or decline await   .
> The tempter of the everlasting steppe.'

'I,' says the poet, ' am like a sailor or traveller, whose business is to go perpetually from place to place, and at his stoppages to sell and buy, and communicate his knowledge to those into whose company he is thrown : so long as he is weather-bound, or any use is to be got from the narration, he will sit and tell you all his travels, just as so long as I am bound by an idea, or there is use in com-municating it, I give you the full benefit of the idea. But as soon as the landwind springs up, the sailor is off; and as soon as my idea is exhausted and told out, so soon as its immediate influence is gone from me, I must go on my way too, and gather new fruits.

Now what has the enunciation of this principle to do with the work of the poem of Sordello ?   In the first place, the very fact of the poet's breaking off the thread of his story to enunciate it, is a proof that that work is, so far as he can make it, true ; that is, he desires to get at the truth in writing it. In the second place, he proposes to do what he does not admit that he can be called upon to do, but means to do out of pure love, that is, he proposes to give to the world his deepest thoughts which have made up his life hitherto, his speculations as to what he will do, or ought to do, hereafter; in the third place, feeling that he has an experience which he ought to impart, he proceeds to give it, and to show how the work of the poem 'Sordello' was prompted by that experience, and in what way Sordello's ideal resembled or differed from his own.

Now the musings which have thus been displayed took place as the poet sat upon a ruined palace-step at Venice: and as he came to this point his eyes fell upon some beautiful Italian peasant girls, poor and half naked, but in the full bloom of beauty, health, and strength. The sight of them, and the blue sky and the bounteous weather, all tending to make him feel happy and contented, roused in his breast, as such influences will in any noble breast, thoughts of other women and men, not so happy and healthy; other skies not so warm and blue, in his own England. These thoughts gradually assume shape, and he seems to see before him a sad dishevelled ghost of a poor woman, who symbolises the poor suffering humanity in England and other countries less favoured than this Italy. This poor ghost symbolises, too, an old ideal of his, which he proceeds to dilate upon. He proceeds in fact to do what he has promised, and give the world

the deepest thoughts which have made up his life
hitherto, his speculations as to what he will do, or
ought to do hereafter, and to show how the work
of the poem ' Sordello ' was prompted by past
thoughts of his life, and in what way Sordello's ideal
resembled or differed from his own.

' Long ago,' he says, ' when I was young, I desired
that all men should be happy, should have power
and riches and health. Gradually I came to see
how impossible this was; and when I left England,
and came to Italy, the magic weather and the
glorious sights and sounds dulled my sense of
sympathy, and dazzled my eyes, and I seemed to
forget what I had once desired for mankind. But
to-day as I looked, the very beauty and health of
the women I looked at, the glories of Venice
round me, recalled to my mind that old dream of
mine, and caused me to feel a pang as if I had
been unfaithful. But on looking deeper, I discover
that perhaps I have not been so faithless after all.
It may be that the beauty of the life around me
has changed my views; but at any rate I will now
take up this old ideal and speak of it, and try to
trace how we may adapt it to actual circumstances
and make the best of what is ; for though this ideal,
so long neglected, has become worn and faded, it
is still an old love, and in its weariness and squalor

is dearer to me than ever. That is, humanity, which I once loved **for what** they might **be, is** dearer far **to** me now than ever, not for what they might be, but for what they are, sinners all, wretched, **starving.**

'**Alas!** I see now (what Sordello has yet to see), that there **is** so little happiness to be got out of the world, that do what we will we cannot share it amongst all. Then what can we do? What shall we do? Shall we try to give happiness to a score, and leave the rest, thus establishing a claim to **the** same happiness for all men? Here, under the influence of **the** Italian weather, **I** will do this; I will say that I have grown wiser; that it is useless my asking for **all** men **to** be made kings and poets; all that I ask is that each may have strength and **health.** I see strength and health round me, and nothing more; and I come to the conclusion that all we can do **is** to say, since these have health and strength, all who are ill and weak have a right to it. But at this point I feel a pang of unfaithfulness again; is not **this** rather a summary, comfortable way of disposing of the question? As I think of this, I see again the miserable thousands, I see again the hope I had which would make them all happy. That hope seems to come **to** me reproachfully again like that worn-out neglected mistress. Can I

not do something then to still this awkward conscience of mine? Can I not finish some work
towards spreading happiness? or at any rate towards
making people see that they cannot alter the first
order, and that even by mere kindly allowance to
their fellow-men they can do great good?

'Alas! my poor worn-out mistress,' cries the poet,
addressing his old ideal in that shape, 'you find me
baulked even of this small hope of making people
at least healthy and strong; what wonder then if
you mistrust my perseverance? You are worn and
faded; but I have not lost my faith in you. And
truth to say I love you more now, than when I
hoped you would be a queen, and all that I could
desire.

'For poor humanity will urge its claims, and is
never ashamed of pressing them too often; my
ideal, if it be a true one, sticks to its master inde-
fatigably, and though bruised and beaten and half
naked, is too much a part of him to deny him.'
That is, let a man go through ever so many
changes, if he has once held any idea which has a
spark of honesty in it, that idea, however ridiculous
it may come to look, is always dear to him as the
worn-out mistress of his early love. He, if he be
really true, is ever too ready to remember his debt.
Nay the very distress and sadness of that past

ruined life, increases his passion for it. And as a man who has once loved a woman truly, who perhaps in their early days has loaded her with jewels and presents, and claimed for her the highest place in the land, when they are both older, if she through no fault of his has become poor and neglected, will then out of his gathered experience try to make her at least comfortable and happy, though his early dreams of queenship are gone and dead—so does the poet deal with this ideal of his, which he has utterly failed to realise in its majesty, but which perhaps he may bring to some use and comfort even now.—Seeing that he cannot make a heaven of earth and make all men chiefs and bards, what will he do now? He says, Let us at any rate see what we can make of life as it stands; what answer we can make to the sanctified ones who are always proclaiming the hopelessness of evil ; can we not say this? Evil exists ; but do not men continue to live in spite of evil? Nay, do not even the worst of men keep their own standard of truth? To this they stick, though they lie to the world; so long as they are true to their own standard they don't care for the standard of the men around them. This is better than having no standard of truth at all. So much for their sense of duty. Then how about their happiness? We see that they are denied a multitude of pleasures simply because, since they will not conform to the rules of the society in which they live, they are denied a multitude of rights; yet they get some one pleasure out of some right which they insist on, and succeed in getting, because the world, which suffers wrong by them, and their perverse views, is not wholly unjust. This is better than if there were no pleasure for bad men at all. But perhaps it will be urged, It may be very well to say that bad men have their conceit of truth, but this does not excuse their badness. Nay, have they any conceit of truth at all? Surely not; for do they not tacitly acknowledge that they are bad and deceitful, in trusting, (as they do) the very world which they make a practice of wronging? To this I reply, they have their conceit of truth, and I will prove them to have it out of the very argument you have used. You say, if these men have their conceit of truth, and believe all the rest of the world to be false therefore, why do they trust the world to which they work evil and wrong? Don't they do so because they think the rest of the world better than they, and therefore more honourable? I say, no; they do it for the very reason that they have their conceit of truth; they do it for the very reason that they think all other men

stupider than they are, that is, they believe that
they themselves alone know the secrets of the
scheme of evil. They argue, in short, that they
have the secret of truth, and all others are wrong ;
that they are obliged to act in defiance of the
world's laws, because these laws are wrong ; that
they carry out the scheme of evil (that is of acting
in defiance of the world's laws) in order that they
may achieve their end, and at last make their
own idea of truth and good triumphant ; and that
since their object is only to be had by working
that scheme of evil, the good which they labour to
produce can only be produced laboriously by working on the ignorance of the rest of the world. This
view at any rate accounts for the mode of life of
most men, and disposes of all evil save the sickness
which is the cause of death; and that evil is not
an evil of life at all. If then, men do really live in
this way, if this is how the world really works ; and
if we can't repudiate our common humanity—our
portion in the common lot—what is one to do ? At
least one can try to make ignorance as small as
possible; one can try by honest means to show
what really is the truth, the true life ; at any rate
this is better than standing idle and proclaiming
impossible remedies as some people do, who vaguely
talk of the "water of life," and each of whom

U

arrogates to himself the conceit that he knows where to find at least a dewdrop of that water.

'These dullards are intolerable; they are as bad and pernicious to the actual moving, working world as a man would have been to the Israelites in their desert journey, if while the whole nation was baked with heat and thirst, he had stood still with folded hands and proclaimed his wonder that anyone need be thirsty when there were plenty of fountains somewhere. At least the man who attempts to make the best of the suffering which exists is better than such idle rascals, even though his efforts are not always directed in the prescribed course of social laws; just as Moses was better than the hypothetical proclaimer of fountains, when he disobeyed a mandate by awkwardly smiting the rock instead of speaking to it. But at this point one of these frothy wiseacres interferes; who is this presumptuous setter up of new creeds; how does he dare to tell us what the office of our life is, and magnify it to absurdity in his optimism? Nay, I rejoin, it is not I who set up new creeds, it is you who would do so; it is not I who can tell you what the office of our life is, nor do I magnify that office unduly; it is you who are always telling us what that office is, and are always jumping to enormous conclusions from very insufficient premises indeed.

Office, forsooth! How can we tell, here on this earth, what our office is? With wrong and failure on every side, with rogues and fools in power and wealth, and honest men and true in obscurity and want, can anyone say that the end and object of life is obtained here? Surely not. We are all of us here on the earth, with varied powers, in perpetual social contact; we are perpetually altering, developing, we never come to a stop till death. What then can we do here? If we cannot each finish our lives to a perfect round, we can surely make use of our daily growth to gain experience, we can surely make use of others' daily growth and glean experience from them. We can in short, since we find ourselves in a crowd of fellow-beings, test each other's power and watch each other's developments, and consider how far we can mutually benefit each other by exchange of the good which our respective faculties are readiest at producing; since on this earth we are only growing, since all we can really do is as it were to watch the construction of an engine out of the various attributes which make up the entire man, let us apply ourselves to do this task as well as possible. When the end comes and we die, then the engine is complete for use; but it is not complete till then; and only then is it complete in so far as the workman

who made it (that is the man himself) has been
earnest and skilful. But is this engine, the complete man, who has been in process of erection all
his life, to be absolutely destroyed at the end of it
like a child's cardhouse ? Is the glorious machine,
all new and ready for action, to be let stand and
become rusty and useless? Surely not. Our
finished being is to be used in another life, where
the work of watching construction will be done,
for the machine is complete, and no more construction is necessary.

'But to revert to this life, and the men in this
world; I have shown what is plainly a man's urgent
duty here. Now although the general principle laid
down is applicable to all, that each should get by
heart and be master of the attributes of all his
fellows, there must necessarily be a large majority
whose daily stress of labour occupies them far too
closely to allow of their looking aside at their
fellows, and a still larger number who have not the
power to perform the function of observing. There
are again a few who possess this power of observing
in a prominent degree; and these are poets, such
as I who speak. We poets then are divided into
three classes; one who sees and says he sees (without describing the *nature* of the thing seen); a
second who describes the *nature* of what he sees; a

third who imparts the gift of seeing the thing, and its nature, to other men. Now I who preach to men the before stated ideal, will further assert that each of these classes of poets or makers is bound to exercise his own functions to the utmost. And as I preach this gospel to poets, I will proceed to put it in practice myself; here are three instances of the power which I claim as one of the third and highest of the three classes I have described.

'So that I glance,' says such an one, 'around,
And there's no face but I can read profound
Disclosures in : this stands for hope, that—fear,
While for a speech, a deed in proof, look here!'
'Stoop, else the strings of blossom where the nuts
O'erarch, will blind thee ! Said I not? she shuts
Both eyes this time, so close the hazels meet!
Thus, prisoned in the Piombi, I repeat
Events one rove occasioned, o'er and o'er,
Putting 'twixt me and madness evermore
Thy sweet shape, Zanze! therefore stoop!'
      'That's truth!'
(Adjudge you) 'the incarcerated youth
Would say that!'
   'Youth? Plara the bard? Set down
That Plara spent his youth in a grim town,
Whose cramped ill-featured streets huddled about
The minster for protection, never out
Of its black belfry's shade and its bells' roar.
The brighter shone the suburb—all the more
Ugly and absolute that shade's reproof
 Of any chance escape of joy — some roof

Taller than they, allowed the rest detect
Before the sole permitted laugh (suspect
Who could,'twas meant for laughter, that ploughed cheek's
Repulsive gleam!) when the sun stopped both peaks
Of the cleft belfry like a fiery wedge,
Then sunk, a huge flame on its socket's edge,
With leavings on the grey glass oriel-pane
Ghastly some minutes more.   No fear of rain—
The minster minded that!   In heaps the dust
Lay everywhere.   This town, the minster's trust,
Held Plara : who, its denizen, bade bail
In twice twelve sonnets, Tempe's dewy vale'—
' Exact the town, the minster, and the street!'
   ' As all mirth triumphs, sadness means defeat:
Lust triumphs and is gay, Love's triumphed o'er
And sad : but Lucio's sad.   I said before
Love's sad, not Lucio : one who loves may be
As gay his love has leave to hope, as he
Downcast that lust's desire escapes the springe :
'Tis of the mood itself I speak, what tinge
Determines it, else colourless—or mirth
Or melancholy, as from heaven or earth.'

' Do you agree to my instances ? Yes! Good.
Then I have vindicated my right, as a poet, to
preach to you, another poet, and have imparted to
you the gift of seeing.   Now, let me beg you to
take another step, and *believe* the sights I see.   If
you decline to believe in what I say I see, because
you cannot see it, you are sinning against the law
I have laid down, which compels you to strive to
the utmost to master all human attributes.   For

what I, a man, have seen, you, a man, may see too, more or less. I may have better opportunities for examination of the subject; but you are not excused from examining what I put in your way, merely because you have not the means of testing my truth by reference to the fountain-head. If, on the other hand, you object that the looking at such a sight as I am obliged to ask you to take on trust is useless, because you cannot turn it to actual tangible result, I admit frankly that its use is not here. Nay I fully admit that for the purposes of this life the men of action are better, who see indeed little, but use that little. But there is another life; and when the greatest poets not only see and tell what they see, but turn their sight to use for themselves and the world, we shall be in heaven indeed. Still you can hardly object to the greatest poets while they are here, using this faculty of seeing what others cannot see; even you will admit that they are only doing what they are bound to do, viz., carrying out the law I have laid down for them. And if they are bound to do this, surely the world's duty is to keep them up to that work, by round abuse if need be.

'So that I bring you round to the subject of my poem, and show you that at least I cannot be abused for neglecting this work which I say we

poets have to do; seeing that I drag to the surface
Sordello's inmost soul which I *have* deciphered,
leaving it to be deciphered by you as best you can.
Not that if you turn and rend me for my work I
shall be vengeful, like Hercules in Egypt: indeed
the true suffrage of one friend is enough for me—

> Yours, my patron friend,
> Whose great verse blares unintermittent on
> Like your own trumpeter at Marathon—
> You who, Platœas and Salamis being scant,
> Put up with Ætna for a stimulant,
> And did well, I acknowledged, as he loomed
> Over the midland sea last month, presumed
> Long, lay demolished in the blazing West
> At eve, while towards him tilting cloudlets prest,
> Like Persian ships at Salamis.   Friend, wear
> A crest proud as desert, while I declare
> Had I a flawless ruby fit to wring
> Tears of its colour from that painted king
> Who lost it, I would, for that smile which went
> To my heart, fling it in the sea, content,
> Wearing your verse in place, an amulet
> Sovereign against all passion, wear, and fret.
> My English Eyebright, if you are not glad
> That, as I stopped my task awhile, the sad
> Dishevelled form, wherein I put mankind
> To come at times and keep my pact in mind.
> Renewed me—hear no crickets in the hedge,
> Nor let a glowworm spot the river's edge
> At home, and may the summer showers gush
> Without a warning from the missel-thrush!

' Thus then, if only for the sake of one or two true

friends, I am glad to have thus put forth my deep ideal of the use of life for men's happiness and the poet's work to that end.'

So the poet resumes his narrative, first entreating his audience not to misconceive his portrait of Sordello, and take him for a devil, who may all the time be a saint, lest they should by such condemnation perchance be damning themselves, as fellow-beings with Sordello.

Now what has this examination of men's and poet's duty in this life to do with the work of the poem of Sordello, and is there any connection in the thoughts here evolved with the thoughts intended to be evolved in the poem itself?

In the first place it is plain that, as already stated, the undertaking to unravel Sordello's soul is an attempt to perform that highest of the poet's duties, the making other men see what he sees in its deepest nature. And is there not an obvious link between Sordello's ideal and that of his narrator?

Sordello saw human nature and tried to display in himself all its attributes without exercising any; that is, he tried the impossible task not merely of showing to men all their deepest attributes in speech, but of actually acting and being all men in all their deepest attributes. The ideal was the same, warped by the egoism of youth. When

Sordello failed in this, finding his means insufficient to his will, he found a prospective opportunity
of influencing men by his actual acquired position
as prince and Palma's husband, and of making
them happy in acting out all their noblest attributes by virtue of that power of his, wedded to his
imagination.   That is, he would now show to men
all their deepest and highest attributes, not only by
his own poetic force, but by inducing them through
his power to exercise those attributes for themselves.   But still all this time he failed to see not
only in all other men, but in his own self, the stern
existence of the common attributes of the fleshly
nature, or despised those common attributes as
clogs to his purpose.   He failed to see what his
biographer sees clearly, that whatever exists must
be used according to its own innate laws and
cannot be disregarded. ' Thus his ideal was plainly
the same with the poet's, only it was not so far
developed.   How it did develop, and in what
direction, has been seen in the ensuing books of the
poem.

EPILOGUE.

In bringing to a close the various thoughts evoked by a few grand utterances, some concluding words will not be out of place.

If at a first backward glance over the whole series of essays, it should appear to the reader that the speculative or religious views in each are inconsistent one with another, it should be remembered that each poem has been treated as a separate effort, as forming by itself, in a quasi-dramatic guise, a distinct train of thought. The train of thought, which was the basis of each poem, must necessarily be treated, in the development of it which has been attempted, as consistent only with itself; and the first duty of the essayist was to preserve, as far as possible, in all his ramifications, the same *principle* of intellectual research as supported the actual poem in hand.

And yet, as will appear more plainly in the following words, there runs through the seeming inconsistency of each theme a thread of unity which supports the whole.

Let us shortly review, and bind together into one, the subjects to which our attention has been directed.

We have been taught, then, how to aspire in our love passion; we have learned the consequences of thwarting intellect, and the sin of checking human love or charity; we have learned too the terrible retributions which overtake little evil doings, and the necessity of using failure as a positive force. We have seen the duty of man to man in checking or avenging evil-doing; we have seen how sexual love, human love, failure and duty, were all united in the grand ideal of Sordello; we have found in the striving of David the manifestation of an attribute, the spirit of prayer, without which neither passion, nor intellect, nor love, are of any avail.

Is there not a strong bond of unity between all these ideas? We see first that a man, as man, may, indeed ought to, develop his natural faculties, as represented by the highest natural faculty of all, the power of a man's love for woman, of a woman's love for man. We learn next that he should extend that power of sexual love, in the wider sense of love for all humanity as such. Then we find that love must not stop here, but must elevate itself to sympathy with and help of intellectual power, whether hidden or revealed.

So much for our broad duties as human beings towards our fellows. We now learn that such being our duties towards the attributes which according to the scheme of our nature must be called good, we have on the other hand to combat and resist evil attributes or impulses wherever we find them: we see not only that there will be divers consequences to undergo, if we fail or sin, but also what those consequences involve both to ourselves and the world. And then we have in 'Sordello' the full fraught history of a life which occupied itself on all the duties we have learned from the other poems, and which gives ample evidences of all possible consequences of failure and wrong-doing. We learn from the thoughts in 'Saul' what is the real mainspring of all effort in this life, whether for duty, love, good, or (relatively to the world) evil. Lastly, we have seen what was the motive which has caused the poet to write all these thoughts, and having seen what are men's duties to each other as men, we learn from him a high scheme of life to be followed by that class which in another life should be supreme rulers, the class of poets, in their capacity as poets.

And in all these struggles of men and women, poets and others, we see incompleteness, and little joy ; desire and little fruition. In each we admire not what they did, but what they tried to do ; in each the failure of the achievement, and not the nature of the thing striven for, moves our pity and wakes our sympathy.

But let us not make the fatal mistake of supposing (what many men without knowing it are apt to suppose) that it is rather than otherwise a grand thing to be unsuccessful, and that success is synonymous with coarseness and charlatanry. If sorrow is greater than joy, and failure more than success, can we not live ? Is it nothing that we have beating hearts, and strong health, if we fail in our passion; or is it nothing that we have love and passion if we fail in intellectual aims ? Surely each man is too often a vexation to himself by reason of his desires ; but of all things the most hateful is that falsest of all false guides, the idealisation of grief or ill success. It so often happens that when a man has plenty and comfort, and wide powers of doing actual good, he thwarts that power by brooding over possible enjoyments, and in seeming honesty of purpose idealising *them* to the utmost. He has, perhaps, failed in love, or in some intellectual scheme : and he straightway erects an idol of his failure, and falls down and worships it, leaving the poor world which has so much really stern sorrow in it to go past wailing or entreating, without moving a finger to help it. He, forsooth, is to be engaged all his best years in lying prostrate before his self-created idol; he, forsooth, is a man of exceptional aims, and specially fine nerves, and must not let his old useless hopes die out lest he should become even as other men, and all his fine nature be coarsened and deadened by the rubbing of the vulgar men and women of the public world. This is the most pernicious form of selfishness; because the subtlety of its insinuations invariably deludes the victim into supposing that he is serving some high end in so abstracting himself from useful work; almost any other form of selfishness has in it some working power, and makes its owner of some actual use.

Then let us take the true lesson, which all these utterances of the poet's have been intended to teach; the lesson which is to be extracted from them and from all others of his works—it is this. Always try to work in the direction of an end which is beyond your power, and get other men to sympathise with and fully understand your aspiration. Such an end is sure to be greater than one which is within your own reach; and is sure, if rightly worked, to command the interest of other men. Never be afraid to admit others to a knowledge of what you desire; never let selfish pride induce you to keep the credit of an achievement all to yourself. If the end be really a worthy one, it must necessarily almost be beyond your grasp; and the more unattainable it is, the more men it will require, the longer time must elapse, before it can be completely gained. And then (to take the instances we have been studying) whether the end be the general idealisation of sexual love, human love, the power of intellect, the utilisation of failure, or the searching out and punishing of evil doing, the same means must be used, the same attribute called into exercise; those means namely, and that attribute, which David and his successors used, and which made up the life of Sordello.

And in trying to draw these conclusions, we are but paying a small tribute to the unwearied efforts of the poet whose works have given us such boundless treasures of thought; we are but acknowledging that in some slight way we have felt the honesty of the purpose of his life and his writings, as plainly set down in his laws for the regulation of poetic effort.

And, to draw one more conclusion before we take a loving farewell of the poet and his works; from all these instances we gain one more proof of the unity of human thought and effort; each for himself has striven towards his own end, and pursued it by a separate path; while the poet, as judge and contemplator, has put down, for the behoof of all, the features and the particulars of life of each striver.

But at the close of the day, all men must find themselves emerging from the great portal of life, and, hand in hand with the poet, whose work is done, must enter a grey negative land, which to some is failure, to some absence of hope, to some joy and rest. All are at last joined together—in suffering, in disappointment, in joy, peace, success; all now march forward, as brothers in a future hope, towards the far off light which beams along the horizon of that gloomy land, and which is the shore of a new country.

In that new country, let us hope, all aspirations are one: in that new country, may the poets realise the dream of Sordello's creator, and reign unchecked in thought and act; may humanity, its hopes and fears, its joys and sorrows, be swallowed up in one perfect love, one perfect power.

LONDON: PRINTED BY
SPOTTISWOODE AND CO., NEW-STREET SQUARE
AND PARLIAMENT STREET

THE GOLDEN TREASURY

SERIES.

Uniformly printed in 18mo. with Vignette Titles by Sir Noel
Paton, T. Woolner, W. Holman Hunt, J. E. Millais, &c. Bound
in extra cloth, 4s. 6d. ; morocco plain, 7s. 6d. ; morocco extra,
10s. 6d. each Volume.

The Golden Treasury of the best Songs and Lyrical
Poems in the English Language. Selected and arranged, with
Notes, by Francis Turner Palgrave.

'There is no book in the English language which will make a **more delightful**
companion than this.'—*Spectator.*
'This delightful little volume contains many of the best original lyrical pieces
and songs in our language, grouped with care and skill, so as to illustrate each
other like the pictures in a well arranged gallery.'—*Saturday Review.*

The Book of Praise from the best English Hymn
Writers. Selected and arranged by Sir Roundell Palmer.

'All previous compilations of this kind must undeniably give **place for** the
present to the "Book of Praise."'—*Saturday Review.*
'It is the most comprehensive and excellent collection that has ever **been made,**
approaching as nearly as one can conceive to perfection.'—*Nonconformist.*

The Sunday Book of Poetry.
Selected and arranged by C. F. Alexander.
'A well selected volume of **sacred poetry.'**—*Spectator.*

The Ballad Book.
A Selection of the Choicest British Ballads. Edited by Wil-
liam Allingham.
'The most perfect "Ballad Book" ever produced.'—*Nonconformist.*

GOLDEN TREASURY SERIES,

continued.

La *Lyre Française.*

Selected and arranged, with Notes, by Gustave Masson, French Master at Harrow School. With Portrait of Béranger, engraved by Jeens.

'We doubt whether even in France itself so interesting and complete a repertory of the best French Lyrics could be found.'—*Notes and Queries.*

The *Children's* Garland from the best *Poets.*

Selected and arranged by Coventry Patmore.

'It has the merit of being the best of its kind, and of having been collected with a definite object and by a competent person. It embodies the union of simplicity with sterling sense and genuine poetry, which a garland of poetry for children ought to contain.'—*Saturday Review.*

The Song Book:

Words and Tunes. From the best Poets and Musicians. Selected and arranged by John Hullah, Professor of Vocal Music in King's College, London.

'A choice collection of the sterling songs of England, Scotland, and Ireland.'
Examiner.

The Poetical Works of *Robert* Burns.

Edited, with Biographical Memoir, by Alexander Smith. 2 vols.

'Beyond all question the most beautiful edition of Burns yet out.'
Edinburgh Daily Review.

A Book of Golden Deeds of all Countries *and all*

Times. Gathered and narrated by the Author of 'The Heir of Redclyffe.'

'We have seen no prettier gift-book for a long time, and none which, both for its cheapness and for the spirit in which it has been compiled, is more deserving of praise.'—*Athenæum.*

The Fairy Book:

Classic Fairy Stories. Selected and rendered anew by the Author of 'John Halifax.'

'A delightful selection in a delightful external form.'—*Spectator.*

The Jest Book:

The Choicest Anecdotes and **Sayings.** Selected and arranged by Mark Lemon, Editor of ' **Punch.** '

' The best Jest Book that has yet been produced. **There is some ring of wit in** every scrap of it, and there is nothing in any page of **the volume to disqualify it** for service on the drawing-room table.'—*Examiner.*

The Adventures of Robinson Crusoe.

Edited, **from** the Original Edition, by **J. W. Clark**, M.A., **Fellow** of Trinity College, **Cambridge.**

' Mutilated and modified editions of this English **classic are so much the rule,** that a cheap and pretty copy of it, rigidly exact **to the original, will be a prize to** many book buyers.'—*Examiner.*

The Pilgrim's Progress from **this** *World to that*

which is to **Come.** By John Bunyan.

' A prettier and better edition, and one more exactly suited for **an** elegant **and** inexpensive gift-book, is not to be found.'—*Examiner.*

Bacon's Essays and Colours of Good and Evil.

With Notes and Glossarial Index by W. Aldis Wright, M.A., **Trinity College,** Cambridge.

' **By far the most** complete, as well as the most elegant, edition we possess.'
Westminster Review.

The Republic of Plato.

Translated **into** English, **with Analysis and Notes, by J. Ll.** Davis, M.A., and D. J. Vaughan, M.A.

Tom Brown's School Days.

By an Old Boy. With Vignette by Arthur Hughes.

MACMILLAN & CO., LONDON.

New Poems.

By Matthew Arnold. Extra fcp. 8vo. 6s. 6d.

St. Paul:

A Poem. By F. W. H. Myers. Extra fcp. 8vo. 2s. 6d.

'It breathes throughout the spirit of St. Paul, and with a singular stately melody of verse.'—FORTNIGHTLY REVIEW.

Goblin Market,

And other Poems. By Christina Rossetti. With Two Designs by D. G. Rossetti. Second Edition. Fcp. 8vo. 5s.

The Prince's Progress,

And other Poems. By Christina Rossetti. With Two Designs by D. G. Rossetti. Fcp. 8vo. 6s.

Dante's Comedy: the Hell.

Translated into Literal Blank Verse. By W. M. Rossetti. Fcp. 8vo. cloth, 5s.

The Return of the Guards,

And other Poems. By Sir Francis Hastings Doyle, Professor of Poetry in the University of Oxford. Fcp. 8vo. 7s.

Shadows of the Past,

In Verse. By Viscount Stratford de Redcliffe. Crown 8vo. 10s. 6d.

Duke Ernest:

A Tragedy; and other Poems. By Rosamond Hervey. Fcp. 8vo. 6s.

BY COVENTRY PATMORE.

The Angel in the House.

2 vols. fcp. 8vo. 12s.

⁎ A New and Cheap Edition, in 1 vol. fcp. 8vo. beautifully printed on toned paper, price 2s. 6d.

The Victories of Love.

Fcp. 8vo. 4s. 6d.

The Lady *of La Garaye.*

By the Hon. Mrs. Norton.   **With** Vignette and Frontispiece.
New Edition, 4*s.* 6*d.*

My *Beautiful* Lady.

By Thomas **Woolner**.   With a Vignette by **Arthur Hughes**.
Third Edition, fcp. 8vo. **5***s.*

Shakespeare's Sonnets and Songs.

Gem Edition.   Edited by F. T. Palgrave.   Vignette by **Jeens**.
18mo. **3***s.* 6*d.*

The Poems *of Arthur Hugh Clough,*

Sometime Fellow of Oriel College, Oxford.   With a Memoir by
F. T. Palgrave.   Second **Edition**, fcp. 8vo. 6*s.*

The Infant Bridal,

And other **Poems**.   By Aubrey de **Vere**.   Fcp. 8vo. 7*s.* 6*d.*

Behind the Veil,

And other Poems.   By the Hon. Roden Noel.   **Fcp. 8vo. 7***s.*

BY THE ARCHBISHOP **OF** DUBLIN.

Poems.

Collected and Arranged **Anew**.   Fcp. 8vo. 7*s.* 6*d.*

Justin Martyr,

And other Poems.   Fifth Edition, fcp. 8vo. 6*s.*

Sacred Latin Poetry.

Chiefly Lyrical.   **Selected** and arranged **for** use.   Second Edition,
Corrected and Improved.   Fcp. 8vo. 7*s.*

BY PROFESSOR KINGSLEY.

Andromeda,

And other Poems.   Third Edition, **fcp. 8vo. 5***s.*

The Saint's Tragedy;

Or, the True Story of Elizabeth of Hungary.   Third Edition,
fcp. 8vo. 5*s.*

Laurence Bloomfield in Ireland:
A Modern Poem. By William Allingham. Fcp. 8vo. 7s.

Romances and Minor Poems.
By Henry Glassford Bell. Fcp. 8vo. 6s.

BY ALEXANDER SMITH.

A Life Drama,
And other Poems. Fcp. 8vo. 2s. 6d.

City Poems.
Fcp. 8vo. 5s.

Edwin of Deira.
Second Edition, fcp. 8vo. 5s.

Ballads and Songs of Brittany.
By Tom Taylor. With Illustrations by Tissot, Millais, Tenniel, Keene, and H. K. Browne. Small 4to. cloth gilt, 12s.

Brother Fabian's Manuscript,
And other Poems. By Sebastian Evans. Fcp. 8vo. cloth, 6s.

BY AUGUSTA WEBSTER.

Dramatic Studies.
Extra fcp. 8vo. 5s.

A Woman Sold,
And other Poems. Crown 8vo. 7s. 6d.

Prometheus Bound, of Æschylus,
Literally translated into English Verse. Extra fcp. 8vo. 3s. 6d.

Blanche Lisle,
And other Poems.
Fcp. 8vo. 4s. 6d.

MACMILLAN & CO., LONDON.